Afro-Blue

Afro-Blue

IMPROVISATIONS IN AFRICAN AMERICAN POETRY AND CULTURE

Tony Bolden

UNIVERSITY OF ILLINOIS PRESS

URBANA AND CHICAGO

Library of Congress Cataloging-in-Publication Data
Bolden, Tony.
Afro-blue : improvisations in African American poetry and culture /
Tony Bolden.
p. cm.
Includes bibliographical references (p.) and index.
ISBN 0-252-02874-0 (cloth : alk. paper)
1. American poetry—African American authors—History and criticism.
2. African Americans in literature. 3. African Americans—Civilization.
4. Improvisation in art. I. Title.
PS310.N4B65   2004
811.009'96073—dc21   2003004991

CONTENTS

PREFACE

ONE NIGHT IN New Orleans about twenty years ago I went to see the Dirty Dozen Brass Band perform at a local bar called the Glass House. Located uptown on Saratoga Street, the bar lay in the heart of a working-class black community. As I recall, the entrance fee was two dollars with a two-drink minimum. Inside, the air was thick with cigarette smoke. I remember feeling cramped. There was little leg space, and the chairs were small and uncomfortable. There was even a local drunk who had to be told that the woman sitting next to me was my wife. But the beauty of the music made me forget these trivialities.

The Dirty Dozen plays what might be called postmodern New Orleans street music. That is, the music is a unique New Orleans style of jazz. The band plays classics like Thelonius Monk's "Blue Monk," but it superimposes the rhythmic structure of New Orleans marching bands on modern jazz melodies. The result is a funky music that retains the complexity of jazz compositions while also compelling one's feet to move. As if to underscore the primacy of dance, the band was accompanied by a cadre of dancers who performed along with the music.

I sat there oblivious to the smoke and cramped conditions, enraptured by the performance that featured, at one point, an eight- or nine-year-old black boy who demonstrated his competence by playing trumpet with one hand. After a stellar performance of Miles Davis's "All Blues," one of the dancers noted my enjoyment and said, "Now *that's* some music. That's some *real* music. I ain't never heard that song befo in ma life—an I'm twenty-three years old—but that's some music."

In addition to testifying to the creativity of the blues idiom, the dancer's comments call attention to the importance of style in African American performance. Though he performed his traditional New Orleans dance (known as the second-line) to the rhythms of a song composed before his birth, he could appreciate it because it was played in a style that he recognized and understood.

The following study is an attempt to sample and improvise upon the concepts inscribed within such expressive forms as the second-line dance. Though many of us have been taught to view such forms as mere entertainment—or, worse, as mindless foolishness—I believe that the second-line, like the bamboula in the antebellum era, contains hidden (black) codes indicating cultural resistance in the repressive New World.

At the same time, I do not claim to address *all* of black poetry. Rather, I am interested in analyzing the politics implicit within the historical conditions that prompt artists to question constructed normality. Before 1980, for instance, scratching records was considered taboo. And yet black and Latino artists transformed this practice into a self-conscious mode of discourse that challenged the dominant culture's attempt to render them silent and submissive. *Afro-Blue* is my attempt to situate black poetry within such practices, to riff antiphonally on the critical writers who have previously performed similar songs, and, finally, to present and represent, in the manner of a collage, how the poetics shaped by the resistive energy inscribed in scatting and scratching did not jes grew. Rather, the funk expressed in Buddy Bolden's horn, the beautiful pain in Billie Holiday's voice, and their interrelationships to what I call blues poetics are comprised of histories that are central to my narrative. Word.

⬧ ⬧ ⬧

Grateful acknowledgment is made for permission to quote from the following poems:

"Blues for Leon Forrest" by Sterling Plumpp. Reprinted by permission of the author.

"Congo Square" by Kalamu ya Salaam. Reprinted by permission of the author.

Excerpts from thirteen poems from *The Collected Poems of Sterling A. Brown,* ed. Michael S. Harper. © 1980 by Sterling A. Brown. Reprinted by permission of HarperCollins Publishers, Inc.

Afro-Blue

Trouble in Mind: Early African American Criticism as a Site of Ideological Conflict

WHEN WILLIAM WEAN HOWELLS wrote that Paul Laurence Dunbar's dialect poems are "'delightful personal attempts and failures for the written and spoken language,'"[1] he was blissfully unaware that his statement would haunt African American poets and their critics like a specter for a century. Howells's patronizing tone reflects a benevolent albeit blatant racist ideology. As Marcellus Blount has said, "Howells's brief essay bears all the trappings of the authenticating preface to the typical slave narrative: the white writer testifies that Dunbar is black, that his Negro ancestry is pure, and that the volume is, as the expression would have it, 'written by himself.'"[2] As the recipient of such a rude compliment, there is little wonder that Dunbar would later tell a friend that Howells had harmed him as a writer. Having been praised for his achievement in dialect, Dunbar feared that he could only satisfy readers by continuing to write in that form. As he explained to his contemporary James Weldon Johnson, "'I've got to write dialect poetry; it's the only way I can get them to listen to me.'"[3]

Dunbar's comments summon the image of young black tap dancers who once performed for passersby on the corners of Bourbon Street in New Orleans. After concluding a performance during which there was invariably a painted smile, the dancer would extend his hat in hand to members of the predominantly white crowd who usually responded by dropping a few coins into it. Like the tap dancers, Dunbar never imagined that his medium could become the basis for the sophisticated artistic expression that he wished to create. Severed from the real-life experiences of black sharecroppers in post-slavery America, Dunbar was unable to question fully the hegemony of Anglo-American culture and was therefore unable to envision alternative notions of sophistication.

In the years since Dunbar's death, critics have expressed strong but conflicting opinions about form in African American poetry. Some have defined form in relation to mainstream literary conventions. Almost invariably, these critics have denounced poets who have experimented with black cultural forms. Others have supported the incorporation of oral/aural forms into literature, while differing among themselves about cultural and/or political issues.

This chapter examines these opposing viewpoints regarding vernacular-based forms in black poetry. I will briefly discuss early critics, such as William Stanley Braithwaite and Benjamin Brawley; then I will focus on essays that specifically address the relationship between vernacular expression and literary style, particularly in relation to poetry, beginning with essays written during the Harlem Renaissance and concluding in 1962 at the dawn of the Black Arts Movement. Central to my discussion will be the problem of hegemony, or what W. E. B. Du Bois called the double-consciousness.[4] I hope to demonstrate that categorical denunciations of black poets who have challenged literary conventions constitute an opposition to the development of an Afro-centric redefinition of modernism as well as a quest for literary authority in terms of that redefinition.

William Stanley Braithwaite, the son of Jamaican immigrants, was the first African American writer to gain a reputation for criticism, which was based largely upon the essays he contributed to the *Boston Evening Transcript* and his annual anthologies of poetry from 1913 to 1929. Although Braithwaite had an affinity for romantic poetry, his personal taste did not preclude his interest in African American culture. He compiled an anthology entitled "The Anthology of Negro Authors: Prose and Verse" but was unable to find a publisher.[5] In one of his earliest essays, "A Grave Wrong to the Negro" (1906), Braithwaite pointed out the racist contradictions underlying stereotypical representations of black folk. "There was never in real life a prototype of the negro [*sic*] of the execrable 'coon song'" or the chicken-stealing preacher (13). Yet "it were better if this country were a nation of chicken-stealers than one of money-thieves, soul-murderers and home-destroyers who are bank and insurance presidents" (13).

Notwithstanding the insight displayed in the foregoing passage, however, Braithwaite was ambivalent about the role of the vernacular in black poetry. Though he understood its capacity to function as a window on the people's psyches and praised James Weldon Johnson's dialect in *Fifty Years and Other Poems,* Braithwaite believed that Johnson's *God's Trombones* was his "least original" book because the poems were "but transcriptions of a speech and imagery that needed no creation" (110). Nonetheless, his criticism established a basis upon which later critics would build. For instance, in his review of *Fifty Years,* Braithwaite anticipates one of Johnson's major concerns in his preface to the first edition of *American Negro Poetry* (1922). Commenting upon the dialect poems, Braithwaite says that they "possess the usual intensity of *pathos* and the usual *humorous* abandon" (46–47, my italics).

While Braithwaite was the first successful African American critic, Benjamin Brawley was the first African American academic critic of major importance.[6] Like Braithwaite, Brawley devoted much of his attention to British literature, beginning to publish criticism in the early twentieth century. However, in 1929, he published the third edition of his most important book, *The Negro in Literature and Art in the United States.* It was originally published in 1910, but the first edition focused more narrowly upon visual art than literature.

In *The Negro in Literature and Art,* Brawley reflects a Darwinian influence and presumes that various types of genius are biologically determined.[7] According to this logic, Brawley identifies aesthetics as the unique gift of African Americans. He cites as evidence the fact that by the early twentieth century African Americans had made contributions in various fields of art: music, painting, and poetry. Even the unlearned peasants on the plantations, according to Brawley, evince a strong appreciation for beauty: "find[ing] no better picture" available, the peasant "will paste a circus poster or a flaring advertisement on the walls" (4).

Despite Brawley's wrongheadedness, he was the first critic to identify a genuine folk tradition, and, albeit with limited success, he attempted to analyze this tradition in relation to black poetry. He points out that Paul Laurence Dunbar's popularity rested in part on his success as a performer of his poetry. After citing "When Malindy Sings" as Dunbar's masterpiece in the dialect form, Brawley goes on to list other poems in dialect form, including "The Party," which "proved unusually successful, specially at readings" (72). Finally, Brawley quotes Brand Whitlock, who comments upon the power of Dunbar's poetic voice: "'That last evening he recited—oh! what a voice he had. . . . I can hear him now'" (70–71). In addition, Brawley recognized the tension between sound-based poetics and literary conventions. Again discussing Dunbar, he says that "the dialect poems suffer by quotation" (71).

Brawley's crude formulations were superseded by James Weldon Johnson, whose famous poem "The Creation" marks one of the earliest successful attempts by a black poet to create serious literature based upon vernacular culture. According to Johnson, the key question for African Americans was how to achieve "intellectual parity"[8] with the larger American culture: "The final measure of the greatness of all peoples is the amount and standard of the literature and art they have produced. The world does not know that a people is great until that people produces great literature and art. No people that has produced great literature and art has ever been looked upon by the world as distinctly inferior" (9). Johnson's concern for intellectual parity, however, misses the point. As W. E. B. Du Bois astutely observed in *The Souls of Black Folk* (1903), the spirituals had few rivals as a moving, emotive form before the twentieth century. So the problem was not the fecundity of black art per se but rather its recognition. In other words, Johnson's assumption that vernacular forms had to be revised to become "great" makes a more insightful critique of popular models of art than black cultural production itself, since ex-slaves exercised little control over the institutions wherein art is theorized and/or distributed.

In his discussion, Johnson presents a panoramic view of various art forms created by African Americans. His basic premise is that black artists have been the primary creators of the art forms that are identified as American. The implication, of course, is that marginalized cultures constitute the real stuff of what later become hegemonic cultures. He argues insightfully that ragtime, like hip-hop today, "is hailed as 'American music'" (11). Similarly, Johnson points out that such black dances as the cakewalk, turkey trot, and eagle rock have been revised in theaters and mainstream American dance. He even calls attention to what might be called the body politics in relation to race, gender, and class when he suggests the resistive element of black folk culture: the banning of the (shim-sham) shimmy.

Johnson makes his most important observation in his discussion of literature. Unlike Brawley, he understood the racist ideology inscribed in much of Dunbar's use of dialect. In his now famous comment, Johnson describes dialect as "an instrument with but two full stops, humor and pathos" (41). At issue here is the problem of representation. There is little dispute regarding Dunbar's ability to capture the sound of the black speaking voice. In fact, his success in his employment of the medium seems to have contributed to the controversy. But since Dunbar believed complex artistic expression and black folk culture to be mutually exclusive, he could not question the hegemony of the dominant culture (recall his "broken tongue" phrase to describe dialect) or develop suitable forms to explore the depths of African American culture. Despite its musicality, Dunbar's dialect often depicts a romantic southern past and reflects a limited view of the various manifestations of black vernacular language and music. Consequently, critics like Johnson attempted to theorize alternatives to dialect, so it is not surprising that Johnson does not employ African American vernacular English in *God's Trombones.*

While Johnson correctly points out the limitations of Dunbar's mediation of the black vernacular, his criticism is not always as clear as his poetry. Like Howells, he cannot distinguish between dialect as literary discourse and specific oral forms that could be used by poets as models for written poetry. Johnson's inability to distinguish between vernacular forms and dialect can perhaps be explained by the fact that, his own "The Creation" notwithstanding, there existed in 1922 few established literary styles that could serve as an alternative to the dialect form. As a critic, Johnson was in the unenviable position of attempting to articulate a poetics for which there were no practitioners. Thus, he is careful not to object to dialect in his call for new poetic forms that elaborate upon vernacular forms to capture the full complexities of African American culture (41). Nine years later, in 1931, black poets had discovered the potential that vernacular forms offer. Johnson realized a clear response to his call for an alternative to the dialect form and praised the accomplishments of Langston Hughes and Sterling Brown, who employed the "authentic speech of the Negro in certain phases of real life" (4).

What Johnson recognized was nothing less than the beginning of a national poetics. However, many early critics did not share his passion for black cultural forms. When Hughes published *The Weary Blues* in 1926, Countee Cullen, who had published *Color* the year before, was among the first to criticize him. In a 1926 review, Cullen writes,

> "Never having been one to think all subjects and form proper for poetic consideration, I regard these jazz poems as interlopers in the company of the truly beautiful poems in other sections of the book. They move along with the frenzy and electric beat of a Methodist or Baptist revival meeting, and affect me in much the same manner. The revival meeting excites me, cooling and flushing me with alternate chills and fevers of emotion; so do these poems. . . . "The Cat and the Saxophone" knocked me completely on the side of bewilderment, incredulity . . . but is it a poem? . . . In the face of accomplished fact, I cannot say this will never do, but I feel it ought never to have been done."[9]

Observe the irony here. Cullen does not deny the effectiveness of Hughes's poetry; on the contrary, he demonstrates a clear understanding of blues poetics. He points out the emotive quality of the poetry and quite appropriately compares the feelings they arouse to a revival meeting. Yet Cullen interprets Hughes's formal innovation as a basis for critique.

At issue here is cultural authority. In the foreword to his anthology *Caroling Dusk,* Cullen outlines the critical standards that undergirded his condemnation of poetry based on vernacular culture. According to Cullen, there should be no distinction between black poets and British poets because the task of black poets is to uphold the British literary tradition.[10] He bases his reasoning on the fact that African Americans are inheritors of the English language. For this reason, black poets benefit more from studying British and mainstream American poetry than straining "atavistic[ally]" for "African inheritances."[11]

Cullen is right to point out the ludicrousness of transposing pre-twentieth-century African forms onto twentieth-century American culture, but there is a crucial flaw in his reasoning. Although he notes the obvious—that black people are speakers of English—he ignores the cultural violence that contextualized the imposition of the language. In other words, there is no opposition between American art and "African inheritances." Cullen's bourgeois politics precluded his ability to understand the value of cultural fusion. Though he presumably abhorred racial atrocities like lynchings, Cullen could not challenge the hegemony of the dominant culture and thereby participate in a more fundamental type of resistance.

A few months after Cullen's review, Hughes defended his efforts in his essay "The Negro Artist and the Racial Mountain." Responding specifically to George Schyler's denial of the existence of African American culture, Hughes compares the legacy of African American ancestry to a mountain that black artists must climb in order to produce genuine art. At the same time, he retaliates against Cullen by signifying upon him in the opening sentence: "One of the most promising of the young Negro poets said to me once, 'I want to be a poet—not a Negro poet,' meaning, I believe, 'I want to write like a white poet'; meaning subconsciously, 'I would like to be like a white poet'; meaning behind that, 'I would like to be white.'"[12]

In foregrounding the problem of the double-consciousness, Hughes identifies a Manichean perspective in the families of privileged blacks who interpret negative behavior as "be[ing] like niggers," while children are encouraged to view white men as models of positive behavior (167). Hughes suggests that such families are veritable incubators of self-hatred. Since they can only view poor blacks with derision, they are not able to see the beauty in the expressive forms they create.

The ironic tone in which Hughes describes well-to-do blacks gives way to a celebratory tone in his assessment of folk culture. But he does not praise poor blacks simply because of their economic status. According to Hughes, working-class blacks "furnish a wealth of colorful, distinctive material for *any* artist because they still hold their own individuality in the face of American standardizations" (168, my italics). Hughes then suggests that black spokespersons bypass valuable opportunities in deemphasizing black culture in their efforts. In so doing, they become mere imposters. "Let the blare of Negro jazz bands and the bellowing voice of Bessie Smith singing Blues penetrate the closed ears of the colored near-intellectuals," he writes, "until they listen and perhaps understand" (172).

Despite the elegance and perspicacity of "The Negro Artist and the Racial Mountain," the question of form in black poetry would require a more in-depth analysis than Hughes was prepared to give. The metaphorical mountains that black artists must climb are not racial but cultural. Though Hughes successfully lampoons the misrepresentation of African American art, he does not expound upon the issues of class and nationality in relation to black poetry. One writer who did address such issues was Alain Locke. While many reviews denounced Hughes's next book, *Fine Clothes to the Jew*,[13] Locke praised the book for "'its open frankness.'"[14] A year earlier, Locke had praised *The Weary Blues* for exactly the same reasons that Cullen criticized it.[15] According to Locke, Hughes's poetry "seems to be saturated with the rhythms and moods of Negro folk life. A true 'people's poet' has their balladry in his veins; and to me many of these poems seem based on rhythms as seasoned as folk songs and on moods as deep-seated as folk ballads. . . . Dunbar was the show-man of the Negro masses; here is their spokesman. . . . Remember—I am not speaking of Negro poets, but of Negro poetry."[16] Although Locke also confuses race with culture, he demonstrates an awareness of opposing camps in African American poetry that already existed in 1926 and thereby anticipates my argument here. In making a distinction between "Negro poets" and "Negro poetry," Locke suggests that poets like Cullen who employ models from mainstream culture in their poetry are African Americans who write poetry. African American poetry, however, refers to verse that attempts to capture or evoke some aspect(s) of black culture in the writer's poetic style. But while Locke's distinction is faulty, and his failure to account for the possibility of a combination of forms reveals a limitation of his vision, the distinction is important because it is perhaps the first recognition of the competing conceptualizations of African American poetics.

More specifically, Locke's distinction suggests that he understood that a national poetics must be predicated on black expressive forms because they are veritable storehouses of styles that can be appropriated for literary discourse. The obstacle that has prevented black writers from adopting this point of view, according to Locke, is the bugaboo of class politics. In a 1936 essay, "Propaganda—or Poetry?" Locke argues that African American poets after World War I protested racial discrimination and attempted to promote group solidarity based on race.[17] But while this marks a significant improvement upon the vision of eighteenth-century poets like Phillis Wheatley, Locke states: "for a long while it was quite possible for the Negro poet and writer to be a rebel and protestant in terms of the race situation and a conforming conventionalist in his general social thinking. . . . The average Negro writer has thus been characteristically conservative and conformist on general social, political and economic issues, something of a traditionalist with regard to art, style and philosophy, with a little salient of racial radicalism jutting out in front."[18] Claude McKay's poem "If We Must Die" provides Locke with a case in point. According to Locke's standards, the poem is problematic because the virulent opposition inscribed in it is trapped within the dominant culture's ideology of form.[19]

In contrast, Locke felt that Sterling Brown's poetry reflected a sense of cultural maturity. In his essay "Sterling Brown: The New Negro Folk Poet" (1934), Locke suggests that the key to Brown's success in *Southern Road* is his ability to capture the folk when they are conversing among themselves. Locke correctly points out that Brown is able to reveal the complexity of the folk experience to readers through the medium of the people's own speech patterns.[20] In Brown's work, readers do not see the kind of minstrels that occupy Dunbar's poetry but rather thinking individuals who negotiate their lives with their own homespun wisdom. In this way Locke suggests that Brown's poetry is an effective form of propaganda because it illustrates the people's material conditions in a discursive form that they might recognize themselves.

In his critical essays, Brown is equally supportive of a vernacular-based poetics. Indeed, his concern for an African American aesthetic is a recurrent theme in his essays. In "Dunbar and the Romantic Tradition" (an essay included in his 1937 survey *Negro Poetry and Drama*), Brown addresses the controversy over dialect form. Brown observes that pre–World War I poets who rejected the dialect form were correct in their "refusal to perpetuate stereotypes of Negro life and character."[21] But Brown points out that in their quest for an alternative to dialect, few poets "challenge[d] the existing order" (58), and most of them rejected identification with African American peasants and workers: "The pressure of their times inclined them to stifle originality: the Negro leader or spokesman excelled in proportion to his resembling the favored white elite" (58). Turning his attention to modern black poetry, Brown calls Hughes's "The Cat and the Saxophone (2 A.M.)" a "metrical revolt" (78).

Needless to say, Brown disagreed entirely with Cullen's ideas about poetry. Brown believed, as did Locke, that literature could be used as propaganda to challenge hegemonic discourses. However, he does not specifically address the issue of nationality or the relationship between art and politics. Though these problems are subtexts in his essays, Brown focuses on the creative process itself and follows Johnson in formulating critical ideas based upon his own revisionary process. But while Johnson was ambivalent about the black speaking voice, Brown suggests that such ambivalence reflects the poets'—not the people's—incapacities. In his now famous statement, Brown writes: "Dialect, or the speech of the people, is capable of expressing whatever the people are. And the folk Negro is a great deal more than a buffoon or a plaintive minstrel. Poets more intent upon learning the ways of the folk, their speech, and their character, that is to say better poets, could have smashed the mold. But first they would have to believe in what they were doing. And this was difficult in a period of conciliation and middle class striving for recognition and respectability" (43).

Note the unsubtle attack on Cullen and Johnson for their statements regarding the limitations of African American vernacular English as a poetic language. What is particularly interesting here is Brown's clear implication that class politics barred a flourishing of poetry based upon the African American oral tradition. Brown points out that black poets' disassociation from the black peasantry led to their attempt to profit from the commodification of dialect, which in turn resulted in an inability to perceive its limitations as a form of literary discourse. Since they did not "believe in what they were doing," observes Brown, these poets felt no compulsion to study black cultural forms to detect the wisdom inscribed therein. Consequently, poets wrote either banal imitations of traditional poetry or misrepresentations of black culture.

Brown's essays suggest that the most astute approach to the problem of African American poetics is to call into question the assumption that Western literature and black cultural forms are binary opposites. Brown realized

that the whole notion of poetry could be reconceptualized if poets could fuse
the European idea of written literature with the styles of black oral forms.
By incorporating the technology of the dominant culture into the implicit
poetic styles of African American culture, Brown believed that poets could
create a radical poetics that could resist and counter misrepresentation: "I
became interested in folklore because of my desire to write poetry and prose
fiction. I was first attracted by certain qualities that I thought the speech of
the people had, and I wanted to get for my own writing a flavor, a color, a
pungency of speech. Then later I came to something more important—I
wanted to get an understanding of people, to acquire an accuracy in the portrayal of their lives."[22]

Richard Wright also envisioned literature as an effective form of propaganda. But while Brown merely implied the political ramifications of literature, Wright, like Locke, foregrounded the issues of class and nationality. Unlike Locke, though, Wright's participation in the Communist party led him
to view his theoretical formulations as strategies for class struggle. And yet
his position is more difficult to pinpoint because it seemed to change in his
later years. Houston Baker has criticized Wright as an assimilationist critic.[23]
However, the term "assimilation" connotes a conservatism that does not describe Wright's vision. I intend to demonstrate that an accurate reading of
Wright's later ideas reveals an outline for an internationalist, hybrid literary
practice that championed the cause of global democracy.

In his 1937 essay "Blueprint for Negro Writing," Wright echoes many of
the ideas of Locke and Brown. Suggesting that black writers "accept the nationalist implications"[24] of African American culture, Wright lays the ground-
work for a vernacular-based poetics by suggesting that the black oral tradition reflects a distinctive African American culture and attempts to fashion a
poetics for black workers. As the title suggests, the essay is really a "blueprint"
for building and mobilizing a black working-class audience. Wright believed
that if black writers understood the oral tradition, they could displace the
black church and "create values" because "the Negro has a folklore which embodies the hopes and struggles for freedom" (318).

However, Wright did not view nationalism as a revolutionary model but
rather a concept that black writers must transcend (320). The irony, he suggests, is that "in order to transcend it, they must *possess* and *understand* it"
(320). Of course, it is now well known that Wright embraced a Marxist vision.
My point here is that it is important to remember that he interpreted nationalism as a component of the American class struggle. When "The Literature of the Negro in the United States" was published in *White Man, Listen!*

(1957),[25] Wright did not focus heavily upon the literary potential of black folk-lore. In his only reference to black English, for instance, Wright contrasts it with the speech of "white people [who] spoke flawlessly" and refers to it as "broken speech." (215). For this reason, Baker terms the essay "assimilation-ist." But though exile may have clouded his vision, Wright's analysis of ver-nacular culture provided a skeleton of the model that Stephen Henderson would later employ in *Understanding the New Black Poetry*.

Dividing black cultural expression into two groups, Wright describes oral forms as "The Forms of Things Unknown" and describes written literature as "The Narcissistic Level." Of the former, he comments pejoratively, "This divi-sion in Negro life can be described in psychological as well as in class terms. It can be said there were Negroes who *naively accepted* what they were, lived more or less *unthinkingly* in their environment, mean as they found it, and sought es-cape either in religion, migration, alcohol, or in what I've called a sensualiza-tion of their sufferings in the form of jazz and blues and folk and work songs" (210, my italics). Obviously, the tone of this passage contrasts sharply with "Blueprint." Note also the determinism in the words "accepted" and "un-thinkingly." In addition, Wright misreads the spiritual "Steal Away," arguing that it signifies "a paradoxical note of defeat" (210). But the term "steal" implies stealth, not subservience. As John Blassingame points out, references to Canaan or heaven frequently signified freedom.[26] It should be emphasized, however, that Wright does not discourage vernacular-based poetry. He illustrates how vernacular forms can serve revolutionary purposes and repeats his idea from "Blueprint" that these expressive forms depict not only the material conditions in which the slaves and their descendants lived but also their responses to them. "Even at the very bottom of Negro life," he writes, "there existed a knowledge of the dual existence they were forced to live" (214).

Thus, the question becomes: what is the source of Wright's ambivalence? My contention is that he envisioned a global audience for a radical interna-tionalist poetics framed in a Marxist paradigm to address the concerns of all marginalized peoples. In such a revolutionary movement, African Americans would be "the most representative voice of America and of oppressed people anywhere in the world" (226). Where Wright had wanted to bridge the gap between black workers and writers in 1937, in 1957 he theorized a link that ex-tended beyond national borders. He did not emphasize vernacular culture be-cause he underestimated the problem of hegemony in colonial situations. Since hegemonic discourse represses and/or misrepresents the colonized, any viable notion of a radical poetics must necessarily address the problem of form.

Baker's statement that Wright applauded "the vanishing of Afro-American expression qua Afro-American expression"[27] is technically correct, but it fails to consider the dynamic nature of the black oral tradition and the creativity of black writers. Whereas oral performers used rhyme in the dozens and signifying, for instance, hip-hop performers today revise traditional ballads and the soul music of the 1970s by creating rhyming narratives that function like instrumental solos over the beats. Wright did not discourage writers from employing vernacular forms in literary discourse; he simply ignored the question of form because he was most concerned with content. He cites Margaret Walker's "For My People" and Brown's "Old Lem" as examples of radical poetry. Wright also states that African Americans created "original contributions in terms of form and content" (210) and that his "conviction [is] that the subject matter of future novels and poems resides in the lives of these nameless millions" (212).

Wright understood that the demise of legal segregation would have an impact upon African American culture. Though he misinterpreted the ramifications of the 1954 Supreme Court decision, he was correct in his prediction that the increased contact between blacks and whites would yield new forms. "At long last," Wright writes, "maybe a merging of Negro expression with American expression will take place" (228). While this statement can be read as assimilationist, I would argue that Wright is actually advocating a more fluid process of creolization. As poets such as Kamau Brathwaite and Jayne Cortez (whose work I will discuss in detail in chapter 6) have demonstrated, an infusion of European culture does not necessarily constitute a negation of black culture. Rather, the question hinges upon the terms of cultural borrowing.

Baker's charge of assimilationism can be more aptly brought against J. Saunders Redding, whose 1939 publication, *To Make a Poet Black,* marked the first attempt to provide a detailed analysis of African American poetry. Although Redding acknowledges the radical politics in which black poetry is engaged, he expresses discomfort about vernacular-based poetry.[28] He writes from the premise that black writers have produced literature in order to promote the cause of liberation, but he demonstrates little concern for the problem of class. Consequently, his analysis is problematic in several respects. Like Cullen, Redding sees black vernacular forms in negative terms. He mistakes antihegemonic discourse for "buffoon[ery]" (50–51) and assumes that there is such a thing as "pure English" (36).

Redding's faulty logic can be seen most clearly in his comments about form in the Harlem Renaissance and his reading of individual poets. He effectively illustrates the mindset that prevented Renaissance poets from creating new forms but fails to recognize the negative implications of such a vision. Observe his explanation, particularly his notion of "common sense": "In his anxiety and relief he did not reflect that he was pouring new wine into old bottles. . . . He was afraid of being a fad, the momentary focus of the curiosity of dilettantes, charlatans, and student sociologists. It was common sense for him to attempt to establish himself on something more solid than the theatrical reputation of Florence Mills. . . . New forms were faddish froth" (106). Despite his concern for new forms, Redding is curiously ambivalent toward vernacular-based poetry. In his discussion of Johnson's *God's Trombones,* he commends Johnson for his advancement beyond the dialect form. Citing Johnson's preface as an important landmark in African American aesthetics, Redding notes "Johnson's acknowledgement of his debt to the folk material, the primitive sermons, and the influence of the spirituals" (122). According to Redding, the importance of *God's Trombones* stems directly from its formal revision of the black sermon form.

But in his analysis of Hughes's experiments with blues culture, Redding reveals an arbitrary critical methodology buttressed by conservative politics. He praises Hughes's ability to evoke "black soul" (115), but he undercuts his argument by rejecting the artistic models that arouse such feelings. "Certainly none of the Blues," Redding writes, "no matter how full of misery, and none of the Shouts, no matter how full of religion, ever get beyond a certain scope of feeling. He can catch up the dark messages of Negro feeling and express them in what he calls 'racial rhythms,' but it is as the iteration of the drum rather that the exposition of the piano. He feels in them, but he does not think" (116). One is reminded here of Johnson's implication in his preface regarding the purported limitations of black vernacular English. Redding, like Brawley and Cullen, sees little potential in the blues because he considers the blues as a limited, "superficial" form (120).

Needless to say, Redding's position is reactionary. While folk forms are not ipso facto revolutionary, they have a unique potential for revealing the material conditions in which the people live, as well as their psychological and emotional reactions to these conditions, because they are produced by the folk themselves. But for critics to fully appreciate the political implications inscribed in vernacular forms, they must question traditional Western culture as the axis of human development. Since Redding was a classic assimilationist, he could only envision social change—and a poetics that promoted it—in terms of bourgeois ideology. Thus, he criticizes "the iteration of the drum" in favor of "the exposition of the piano" (116). It should be noted, however, that the drum, too, is capable of complexity. He resorts to nostalgia, calling for black writers to return to the South because black lore has "arisen from a loving bondage to the earth" (124), but ignores the "bondage" that black migrants sought to escape by pouring into America's cities.

In the 1950s few black critics wrote about poetry. Two women who did were Margaret Butcher and Margaret Walker. In her book *The Negro in American Culture,* Butcher focuses on content and does not take a position on form. However, Walker addresses the issue in an essay entitled "New Poets," where she discusses African American poetry from the Harlem Renaissance through the 1940s. Using her sketch of the 1920s as a backdrop, Walker analyzes the poetry of the 1930s and 1940s in detail. Like Wright in "The Literature of the Negro in the United States," she neither discourages nor encourages orally based poetry. Yet despite her formal revisions of black folk forms in *For My People,* she is unable to question the hegemony of traditional notions of craft in her critical essay.

Walker sees a dichotomy between the poetry of the 1930s and 1940s. She interprets the earlier poetry in terms of its radical content and focuses upon form in the later poetry. But while there are certainly differences in style between the two periods, Walker's opposition ignores important poetic achievements. She correctly points out that Brown's "'Slim Greer Series' are some of the finest [ballads] in the annals of American poetry."[29] However, she reads "Old Lem" as merely an expression of social protest and ignores Brown's representation of the black voice and his revision of the slave secular (which I will discuss in detail in chapter 3). Similarly, Walker cites the last two stanzas of her own "For My People" as protest poetry but ignores the creativity of her imagery, stanzaic structures, and use of repetition. Finally, while Walker rightly celebrates the craftsmanship of Robert Hayden's "Middle Passage" and "Runagate Runagate," which were published in 1945 and 1949, respectively, she ignores the radical vision that shapes the poetry.

Like Wright, Walker interprets internationalism in Eurocentric terms (95). Responding to "the long hue and cry of white writers that Negroes as poets lack form and intellectual acumen" (97), she comments that "the new poetry has universal appeal coupled with another definite mark of neo-classicism, the return to form" (96). Note that the word "return" suggests reaction, not progression. It is ironic that Walker's Eurocentric model of universalism prompts her misreading of Myron O'Higgins's poetry. After defending Gwendolyn Brooks against the charge of obscurantism, Walker suggests that the following passage by O'Higgins is more deserving of the criticism:

"But that day in between
comes back with two lean cats
who run in checkered terror
through a poolroom door
and bolting from a scream
a keen knife marks with sudden red
the gaming green
. . . a purple billiard ball
explodes the color scheme." (98)

A careful reading of the passage demonstrates that Walker misses an opportunity to identify an experimental poetic style. While there is certainly ambiguity here, the poem reflects an attempt to create poetry that fuses modernist techniques with language that is particularly resonant in African American culture.

The passage ostensibly describes a fight between "two lean cats"—that is, slender black men in a poolroom (recall Hughes's "The Cat and the Saxophone"). Yet it is really a poetic illustration of urban marginalization. The phrase "in between" in the first line suggests the confinement of ghetto reality. The checkers image reinforces the idea in the previous line by suggesting the surreality of a color-coded society and foreshadowing the bleeding that will occur. The "scream" is what I call a term of (re)memory: while it refers here to pain from a knife wound, the term has been used to describe the sound of black musicians who interpret the culture instrumentally. O'Higgins skillfully employs irony in his use of poolroom symbolism. Though the men are victims of a "color scheme," they do not understand that the implications of pool rules reify white supremacy. The object of the game, of course, is to use the white cue ball to knock the black eight ball into a pocket. The explosion image suggests a gunshot. But rather than "explod[ing] the color scheme," O'Higgins suggests that the men have been constructed into social subjects who do not detect many of the mundane manifestations of racial politics, so they unconsciously follow the plans that the ruling class has created for them.

O'Higgins's attempt to reconcile modern literary conventions with the black oral tradition anticipates the concerns of Amiri Baraka. Writing at the dawn of the Black Arts Movement in 1962, Baraka, then LeRoi Jones, repeats Johnson's call for a poetics informed by Afro-vernacular culture, foreshadowing many of the ideas that became current during the period. Like his Howard University mentor, Sterling Brown, and like Alain Locke, Baraka astutely identifies the problem of hegemony as the main obstacle to a national literature:

> To be a writer was to be "cultivated" in the stunted bourgeois sense of the word. . . . It had nothing to do with the investigation of the human soul. It was, and is, a social preoccupation rather than an aesthetic one. A rather daring way of . . . gaining prestige in the white world for the Negro middle class. And the literary and artistic models were always those that could be socially acceptable to the white middle class, which automatically limited them to the most spiritually debilitated imitations of literature available.[30]

What is interesting here is Baraka's position regarding white literary models. While he is now criticized for the racial chauvinism of the Black Arts Movement, the Baraka of 1962 does not attack black writers for selecting Western models per se. Rather, his charge is that many black writers have created a vapid literature because of their inability to question bourgeois ideology and because of their obfuscated view of art. Since they have mistaken social "cultivat[ion]" for art, they are unable to see the value of writers like James Joyce and Herman Melville and musicians like Bessie Smith and Charlie Parker.

Baraka also echoes Wright's 1937 idea that black writing should be meaningful to working-class African Americans. He points out that popular culture produces most black cultural heroes. However, he is more specific in his discussion of the gap between writers and working-class black people. According to Baraka, the people feel alienated by their writing, and this has prompted their preference of athletes, particularly boxers like Jack Johnson and Sugar Ray Robinson, over literary artists (109). The implication is clear. In order to make literature more meaningful in the everyday lives of African Americans, writers must create a literature that more closely resembles their expressive forms.

Yet Baraka does not call for a romanticized version of African art but one informed by an African-derived sensibility that constitutes a genuine alternative to the literature championed by the literary establishment:

> Africanisms still persist in the music, religion, and popular cultural traditions of American Negroes. However, it is not an African art American Negroes are responsible for but an American one. The traditions of Africa must be utilized within the culture of the American Negro where they actually exist, and not because of a defensive rationalization about the worth of one's ancestors or an attempt to capitalize on the recent eminence of the "new" African nations. Africanisms do exist in Negro culture, but they have been so translated and transmuted by the American experience that they have become integral parts of that experience. (111)

Though he had not in 1962 attempted the formal experiments for which he is now famous, Baraka provides a blueprint for a blues poetics. He does not mention the importance of style specifically, but he clearly implies it when he suggests that black art should reflect the people's emotional responses to the American experience (109). Note the reference to "Africanisms." The "transmut[ations]" that Baraka refers to bear a striking resemblance to Brown's comments regarding the black voice. Like Brown, Baraka suggests that "better poets" can create new American literary forms if they can develop a revolutionary consciousness that will enable them to understand the potential of these forms.

Baraka's blueprint for a blues poetics is important because it anticipates the later emphasis upon jazz as a formal model of performance as well as a source of inspiration. At the same time, it anticipates the strident tones of the debate over black poetic form. Though Baraka is not prescriptive here, many writers became quite rigid in their conceptualizations of nationality, and this ultimately undercut some of the effectiveness of the movement. To engage in a radical—and even didactic—poetics is one thing. To insist or imply that all others must follow suit or risk excommunication is quite another.[31] In any case, it is important to remember that there has never been harmony among critics of black poetry. Notes of discord were trumpeted as early as 1922 when Johnson criticized dialect. But as Cheryl Wall has suggested, the debate actually started with poets themselves, and the first rumblings were emitted when Dunbar referred to dialect as a "jingle in a broken tongue."[32]

2 Meditations: Black Arts Criticism and Cultural Nationalist Aesthetics

PERHAPS THE MOST SALIENT feature of Black Arts criticism is its recurring theme of national liberation, which was usually framed within the context of cultural nationalism.[1] Black folk had been disfranchised as a racial group, so it seemed only logical for critics to theorize injustice on the basis of race. As Jennifer Jordan argues, "The sight of police dogs biting defenseless children, and King's, and even Kennedy's, bloody finales, frozen on front pages and incessantly reenacted . . . sent Black folks into the streets."[2] Since Black Arts poets experimented with new forms, many critics discovered that conventional approaches to criticism were no longer functional; new models were needed to illustrate the immense potential within Afro-vernacular culture, the wellspring for much of Black Arts poetry. The avant-garde pianist Cecil Taylor could have spoken for poets and critics alike when he said, "'Right away when they talk about music they talk in terms of what music is to them. They never subject themselves to, like, what are Louis Armstrong's criteria for beauty, and until they do, then I'm not interested in what they say.'"[3]

Taylor's comments cut right to the core of the either/or logic that is endemic to the process of marginalization. Having recast the medieval Wild Man as the racial other in the modern world, the Founding Fathers of America continued to employ what Hayden White calls "'the technique of self-negation.'"[4] "Who are we?" asks Charles Mills, parodying the voice of the colonizer. "We are the non-savages."[5] An important criterion of nonsavage/personhood status in the Enlightenment was beauty. Observe the following description of blacks in the 1798 American edition of the *Encyclopaedia Brittanica:* "'A short, broad, flat nose, thick lips, small ears, ugliness, and irregularity of shape, characterize their external appearance. The Negro women have the loins greatly depressed, and very large buttocks, which give the back the shape of a saddle.'"[6] Here the black body is at once a sign of domestication and deformity as well as a site of white male sexual pleasure and exploitation. Which is to say, blackness, as an ideological construct of the West, created a subhuman species that could then justifiably be treated differently from nonsavages/persons.

Taylor's comments strike at the very foundation of Western epistemology. His refusal to regard traditional Western aesthetics as the sole locus of artistic theory suggests a politicized consciousness wherein the colonizer's either/or logic is violently dismantled. Yet it is important to bear in mind that Taylor's position was hardly an anomaly. Rather, the Black Arts Movement was a national movement in which politicized cultural workers of various sorts lent their talents and/or critical insights in support of black people's right to "define the world," as Larry Neal put it, "in their own terms."[7] So while writers and musicians were at the forefront in the struggle over black representation, visual artists were also engaged in opposition, as Lorenzo Thomas points out: "Even visual artists such as New York's Joe Overstreet and the Africobra group in Chicago produced images that consciously dismantled and defused the racial stereotypes imbricated in both mainstream and African American cultural tradition while promoting an innovative interpretation of African aesthetic values and racial self-respect."[8] Hence, James Brown's appeal in "Say It Loud (I'm Black and I'm Proud)."

Taylor's critique of Eurocentric critics points up the symbiotic relationship between hegemony and ideology. Rather than asking what is African American art, the more pertinent questions are, *Who constructs the parameters in which black art is conceptualized? And why are some models privileged over others in society?* From my vantage point, Louis Althusser provides the most cogent response. Extending Karl Marx's concepts in *The German Ideology,*[9] Althusser argues that the class that controls the wealth in society also exercises power over the distribution of cultural production: "The class struggle is thus expressed in ideological forms. . . . But the class struggle extends far beyond these forms, and it is because it extends beyond them that the struggle of the exploited classes may also be exercised in [these] forms . . . and thus turn the weapon of ideology against the classes in power."[10] The dominant class thereby represents its interests in universal terms, naturalizing its privilege to facilitate the (mis)representation of political opposition as inherently irrational. Black Arts critics demonstrated their understanding of the power differential in relation to academic critics by contesting the misrepresentation and/or erasure of black poetry, that is, the manifestations of the nexus between colonization and ideology, but neglected to distinguish between the objective of self-determination and the theoretical construct of cultural nationalism. Since critics assumed that the fundamental problem in America was racism, it followed logically that the only viable solution lay in black solidarity.

But if nationalism fueled the fire of Black Arts criticism, it also helped pour the ice water to cool it. Angela Davis and Elaine Brown,[11] who were both active in the Black Panther party, have pointed out the patriarchal nature of the Black Power movement. Moreover, Marx notwithstanding, readers familiar with W. E. B. Du Bois's *Black Reconstruction* would have known that in America race functions as a black/brown mask that conceals the international problem of class. Consequently, many Black Arts critics display great vision regarding racism and the centrality of vernacular culture to the new black poetry but demonstrate less insight in their strategies to address the underlying economic basis of racism.

Much of the antipathy toward a class-based analysis of race stemmed from the complex historical relationships that blacks have had with white-dominated leftist organizations. While the Communist party had championed the Scottsboro Boys and supported black workers like Hosea Hudson and tenant farmers like Ned Cobb in Alabama in the 1930s, Commmunists also disrupted a conference chaired by A. Philip Randolph in Harlem wherein workers demanded an eight-hour day, a five-day work week, and public works for the participants.[12] There was also the example of Richard Wright, who, after initially viewing the party as Eurocentric,[13] eventually joined, only to detect pervasive blindness regarding race among party members that led them to view Wright as an enemy to black workers: "'I [knew] that if they had held state power I should have been declared guilty of treason.'"[14]

Such myopia can still be observed in some contemporary Marxist writing. In an article on the black radical tradition in the early Communist party, Susan Campbell cites the cartoon artist Robert Minor as a white Communist who gave "detailed attention to Black American issues"[15] during a period when Vladimir Lenin was chiding American Communists for avoiding questions related to African American national liberation. Quoting Minor describing his role in the party, Campbell argues that he was "an outstanding example of one who grasped the importance of the Negro question and who devoted much attention and study to the history and social condition of the Negro people."[16] But although Minor did attack such atrocities as lynching in his work, his notion of race reveals a perspective that is barely distinguishable from Ku Klux Klan propaganda. In *"PUGILISM IN EXCELSIS:* The Grinning Negro as He Appears to Robert Minor," Minor depicts the heavyweight champion Jack Johnson as a smiling minstrel figure with the proverbial thick lips. In front of him lay what are presumably human bones.[17]

Black Arts writers were caught in a paradigmatic bind. Like many black artists and intellectuals before them, they were ambivalent toward white intellectuals. In his *Autobiography of LeRoi Jones,* Amiri Baraka recalls the Progressive Labor party's betrayal of a black activist. Rather than coming to his defense, the organization, according to Baraka, left him in jail "to rot" and expelled him as "a nationalist.'"[18] So although most Black Arts writers were painfully aware of the contradictions between black liberation and capitalism, their skepticism toward Marxists led them to marginalize class issues, which in turn deprived them of important opportunities to develop adequate theoretical tools to build a genuinely revolutionary conceptualization of the function of race in capitalist society.

One reason underlying this arrested development concerns the vicious assault upon the Civil Rights movement in the South and the Black Power movement in larger urban areas: the murders of Malcolm X and Martin Luther King Jr. as well as the Black Panthers Bobby Hutton and Fred Hampton in Oakland and Chicago, respectively. Given the foregrounding of praxis in the Black Arts Movement, the lack of a viable political movement was indeed a severe blow to Black Arts writers. More fundamentally, though, Black Arts writers' espousal of cultural nationalism betrayed an epistemology wherein experiential knowledge was often emphasized at the expense of conceptual knowledge and/or theory. As Baraka points out, there was considerable confusion regarding politics:

> I had no formal definition of cultural nationalism. I didn't even correctly know what it was. . . . Some of us were influenced by the Yorubas because we could understand a connection we had with Africa. . . . After so much exposure to white women, the graceful dress of the sisters in their African look, with their hair natural, turned us on. . . . Oserjeman . . . practiced polygamy, and certainly for some of us who were used to ripping and roaring out of one bed and into another, this "ancient custom of our people" provided a perfect outlet for

male chauvinism. All of the various influences focused on white people as en-
emies, devils, beasts, &c., and our thinking fell in perfectly with this.[19]

Baraka's narrative demonstrates in glaring detail the consequences of deemphasizing theory in social/artistic contexts. Without the armament of theoretical knowledge, Black Arts writers often reproduced the very logic of the
system against which they were committed to revolt.

The unlike essays written for an academic audience, Black Arts criticism was
directed primarily to poets and their readers. Consequently, the tone and
tenor of the writing generally reflects the experiential bases of inner-city linguistic practices and constitutes a formulation of critical strategies that simultaneously examine and inscribe the vernacular underpinnings of oppositional black art on a national scale. Cultural organizations included the Black
Arts Repertory Theatre/School (Harlem); Karamu House (Cleveland); Black
Arts West (San Francisco); the Ebony Showcase Inner City Repertory Com-
pany and Watts Writers Workshop (Los Angeles); the Organization of Black
American Culture (OBAC, Chicago); Concept East and Black Arts Midwest
(Detroit); Free Southern Theatre and BLACKARTSOUTH (New Orleans);
Theatre of Afro Arts (Miami); and Sudan Arts Southwest (Houston).[20]

The most controversial aspect of Blacks Arts criticism involved the concept of the black aesthetic. In a defiant manner that was unprecedented, Black
Arts critics posited that African Americans have distinct artistic traditions and
formulated theories to illustrate the beauty of black art. However, "blackness"
proved difficult to define: who defines what is black, and what is the process
by which he or she is accorded the privilege of making that determination?
Part of the problem stemmed from the limited scope of the debates, which
prescribed a single aesthetic rather than a multitude of interrelated aesthetics that reflect and refract transposed African cultures in America in various
geopolitical contexts.[21] As a result, there were problems of regional privilege
as well as masculinism, which culminated in the marginalization of gender
issues. And after ideological rivals like Henry Louis Gates Jr. attacked the Black
Arts Movement on the grounds that it was theoretically unsound and artis-
tically bankrupt,[22] most critics ignored black poetry altogether. Consequently,
questions of audience, poetic language, and cultural autonomy have been
largely occluded. The significance of such questions is intensified when we
consider the paucity of public and financial institutions that publish and dis-
tribute black poetry, the role of cultural production in describing a group's
experiences from its point(s) of view, and black poets' historically troublesome search for an audience.

Black Arts critics followed the example of Langston Hughes's 1926 manifesto "The Negro Artist and the Racial Mountain." They questioned the hegemony of traditional literature and attempted to fashion a poetry based upon oral/aural forms that was designed specifically for the sensibilities of working-class black folk. But in their attempt to create a viable audience, the poets found few models in black literary history. There were the examples of Langston Hughes, Sterling Brown, and Margaret Walker, but postmodern America presented a different backdrop to these young artists, compelling them to search for novel configurations of a black poetics.

At the same time, the poets were keenly aware that other black cultural figures did not share their problem. Preachers and singers, for instance, dwelled in the province of language and performed before ample audiences. Consequently, poets crafted new styles designed to represent the experiences of what black people called "the street(s)"—that is, the most exploited segment of the urban black working class—by appropriating the rhythms, cadences, and lexicon of that group. One of the earliest attempts to analyze the new poetry was made by Haki Madhubuti.

Dynamite Voices[23] was the first book-length study of the new poetry written by a poet. As such, it affords a view of the poetry from the standpoint of a practitioner. The title suggests the conjoining of radical politics and the new aural nature of Black Arts poetry. At the same time, though, Madhubuti's writing illustrates many of the problems related to the poets' adherence to cultural nationalism. For instance, he asserts that the new poetry was based solely upon African American vernacular forms (30), foreclosing any possibility of a formal relationship to Anglo-American poetry and claiming instead that Black Arts poets developed a polyrhythmic poetry whose unique "syntax" bears kinship with "the language of the street" (33), citing as evidence various ways in which the word "muthafucka" (34) has been used by poets to achieve a specifically African American poetic form.

At issue here is Madhubuti's political identification with the black masses. Given the oppositional energy of the expletive in question,[24] his theory of poetics that embraces the anger implied in the term reflects Madhubuti's own defiant albeit problematic stance toward the hegemonic culture (hence, the title of his book, *Don't Cry, Scream*). And yet his quest for a pure, black form undercuts the resistive thrust posed by the Black Arts Movement because it obscures the creolization of African American culture, which, in turn, challenges hegemonic concepts inscribed in such terms as "American" and "literature." One need only point out that popular poets like Sonia Sanchez wrote in a style that was popularized by e. e. cummings.

Madhubuti's analysis of the musical basis of the poetry is also troublesome. For instance, although David Henderson actually sang parts of his poem "Keep on Pushin"[25] (after the song of the same title by Curtis Mayfield and the Impressions), Madhubuti ignores that poem and praises instead Ebon's "Legacy: In Memory of Trane" (42), which is linked thematically to John Coltrane but does not reflect—in print, at least—any of the rhythmic qualities associated with music. Madhubuti's critical limitations stem from a Manichean vision of race. Black critics must write for black people, he advises, because blacks and whites are "natural opposites" (19). Madhubuti's inability to understand racism as a component of an international class struggle leads him to the construction of a hierarchy not unlike that which he purports to raze.

Like conservative critics such as Benjamin Brawley, Countee Cullen, and J. Saunders Redding, Madhubuti believes in a hierarchy of forms in which poetry that is not directly related to "the language of the street" has little value. For instance, he dismisses "Felix of the Silent Forest" as "underworked, over-hipped, psuedo-intellectual" poetry (67), but a cursory glance at the poem reveals Madhubuti's misreading:

> by twilight the clubs released their exotic lures Sylvia's
> Blue Morocco sheds blue light both neon & real on side
> walks and cobblestones between Shabazz Beauty Parlor
> & Denzil's Fabulous candystore
> Velvet Blue drapes hang ceiling to floor and all to be
> seen inside is the spotlighted face of the singer the
> dim blue faces of the music the soloist the master
> of ceremonies—heads truncated in blackness[.] (67)

Madhubuti complains: "[Henderson] speaks of music but doesn't show it in his poetry" (67). Madhubuti's comment suggests a black monolith. While he is correct that the poem is not musical in the way that Madhubuti's best poems are, his implication that black readers cannot appreciate the poem because of its imagistic style is not dissimilar to the traditional positon of Western intellectuals who have theorized blackness as inherently limited. Moreover, the objective of the poem is not to recreate the sound of music but rather to capture the ambience of the nightclub by recording, in a photo-like manner, the actual scenery of the place. Thus, like the academic critics that Black Arts writers abhorred, Madhubuti commits the crucial error of refusing to consider Henderson's poem on its own terms.

Madhubuti's writing also exemplifies the masculinism in the movement, which remains controversial today. Clearly, some of the most important poets of the era were women: Nikki Giovanni, Sonia Sanchez, June Jordan, and Jayne Cortez. But as such writers as Alice Walker would later suggest in stories like "Her Sweet Jerome" and "Everyday Use," the nationalist parameters in which gender was theorized were woefully inadequate. Madhubuti does not reserve compliments for male poets; he speaks positively about the poetry of Carolyn Rodgers and Sonia Sanchez. Rather, it is the *terms* of his compliments that are questionable. Madhubuti quotes the editor and critic Hoyt Fuller, whose language reveals a masculinist sensibility that undercuts the praise he bestows upon Rodgers's poem: "'[her poetry] is like her own frame, slim and straight, and as subtly feminine as a virgin's blush'" (55). Like Fuller (who faced some ostracism because of his homosexuality), Madhubuti describes Rodgers's physical beauty in the guise of analyzing an artistic endeavor. Part of the problem here, again, is that much of black vernacular culture, like American culture generally, is male-centered, and as a product of that culture, Madhubuti had not yet learned to question the narrow framework in which gender is theorized in black culture.

Finally, though Madhubuti rejects academic critics, his criticism reflects the same craft-versus-orality opposition that characterizes most academic criticism of the movement. He criticizes Rodgers's satire of the Black Power movement: "'yeah, i is uh revolutionist / and i belongs to uh revolutionary / group What GOT funDED (!) . . . I write poetry since day befo yesterday'" (58). Madhubuti attacks Rodgers because of such misspellings as "dun." But the poem pokes fun at the contradictions of the movement and at many writers' conflation of typographical tricks with the creation of genuine literature. However, Madhubuti praises a poem written by Rodgers in Standard English that commends the achievements of Hoyt Fuller. According to Madhubuti, "for h. w. fuller" is praiseworthy because it demonstrates a "commitment to craft" (60).

While Madhubuti's critical writing reflects some of the problems associated with cultural nationalism, Carolyn Rodgers herself was one of the period's more insightful critics. Although her criticism of Gwendolyn Brooks's language exhibits intolerance,[26] she wrote several insightful essays about poetry. One of the unfortunate consequences of the critical silence regarding the Black Arts Movement has been the neglect of Rodgers who, as a poet and critic, harbored few reservations about criticizing the weaknesses of the movement. Her importance as a critic stems from her anticipation of the criticism of Stephen Henderson and Henry Louis Gates Jr. Her attempt to create a critical approach designed specifically for African American poetry anticipates Henderson's *Understanding the New Black Poetry;* her concern

for style and her belief that vernacular culture could form the basis for literary criticism anticipates Gates's *The Signifying Monkey.*

Rodgers's essays demonstrate the resistive potential of critical practice
conducted outside of academia. In an essay entitled, "Black Poetry—Where
It's At," Rodgers attempts to describe the diversity in black poetry. She lists
ten different categories:

1. signifying
2. teachin/rappin
3. coversoff
4. spaced
5. bein
6. love
7. shoutin
8. jazz
9. du-wah
10. pyramid[.][27]

It is significant that Rodgers employs vernacular terms in her taxonomy. She
confronts the problem of audience by employing language that is directed to
a popular readership. Of course, the term "popular criticism" is oxymoronic.
Traditional notions of criticism inevitably suggest an elitist activity conducted
for a select group of readers who are presumably the most perspicacious
thinkers in the society. Part of the oppositional threat that Black Arts criticism poses, then, is that it calls into question the fictional opposition of such
terms as "popular" and "critical." Put differently, the problems of cultural nationalism notwithstanding, Black Arts criticism helped foster a consciousness
wherein critical analysis was no longer contained within ivory towers; it was
now alive and well in the concrete jungles of America. Such a criticism can
create a community of writers, general readers, and critics.[28]

Of course, vernacular cultures are always dialogic relative to dominant
cultures, so they are never static but rather always in flux. Thus, writers who
appropriate the vernacular must confront the constant risk of erasure. Rodgers's use of the term "spaced" in her theorizing of Amiri Baraka's poem "No
Matter, No Matter, the World Is the World" provides a test case:

"A broke dead genius
moved on to dust
will touch you one night . . .
. . . and the stacked dust of a gone brother will hunch you
some father you needed who left you[.] . . ."[29]

Though "spaced" is a word that is no longer privileged in vernacular discourse, it is nonetheless useful as a critical tool. As Zora Neale Hurston suggests in her classic essay "Characteristics of Negro Expression,"[30] the black hole[31] of Afro-vernacular culture privileges action words. Thus, nouns are often transformed into verbs. I believe a similar dynamic can be observed in Rodgers's employment of the word "spaced." According to her, a spaced poem involves positive and negative vibrations that return African Americans to "our Egyptian/African forefathers."[32] One is reminded of the Staples Singers' song "I'll Take You There." In this particular mode of poetics, the song/poem serves a function that is akin to the blues tradition in that it transports the reader to a psychic location that is medicinal. One need only attend a spoken word performance today to observe the insight inscribed within Rodgers's model. Even the images themselves suggest the various styles in which black (underground) poets perform today: some shout; some sing/du-wah; some express love; and some pull the covers off via teachin/rappin.

And yet Rodgers's work is not devoid of problems. For her pyramid image "(getting us together / building / nationhood)" sabotages some of the resistive force of the essay. The triangular shape of the pyramid demands that power reside in the hands of a privileged few, while the poor languish at the bottom supporting the base. Despite this contradiction, Rodgers's model challenges the very foundations upon which the mythogology of race has been constructed. The film *Cleopatra* (wherein Elizabeth Taylor stars as queen) typifies the manner in which westerners have made concerted efforts erase the black presence from conceptualizations of Egypt because it exposes the ideological underpinning of the naturalization of white supremacy.

Rodgers's 1971 essay, "Uh Nat'chel Thang—The WHOLE TRUTH—US," represents her best effort for a nonacademically oriented criticism.[33] In her preface she states: "This will not be a traditional prose, poetry or essay piece" (4). While one is hard pressed to distinguish between "prose" and "essay," Rodgers nonetheless presents a style that can accommodate a popular audience: "I can relate to dope addicts and their feelings. Because Nadinola bleaching cream, a straightening comb, an education (educated tongue) and Vaseline for a shininess was my dope" (10). Rodgers's infusion of memoir into her criticism liberates critical practice from the confines of footnotes, lending authority to experiential knowledge, calling into question the mythic opposition between criticism and creativity, and inviting disfranchised writers to engage in similar analyses of the process of their own (re)construction.

Rodgers also attacks the superficiality of the movement, which she interprets as reluctant to study vernacular culture. She points out that excessive attention was placed upon the concept of blackness: "We must not create unrealistic super-black ideals for people to live up to, which are . . . reactionary extreme opposite[s] to super-slave ideals" (7). And although she accepts the false opposition between the English language and "an African emotional experience" (7), Rodgers nonetheless criticizes poets whose only technique was shouting: "Style is important. Style is how. Who you are is how and why you speak" (7). She distinguishes between a politicized art that functions as propaganda and sterile propaganda that pretends to be art. She suggests that a genuinely popular poetics can only be developed by talking to workers in the streets, in bars, and in the sanctified churches "where people shout, and dance and speak in tongues, and the holy ghosts come to visit" (7). Failure to study vernacular culture, she says, culminates in a counterfeit poetics: "After all, there are only so many ways you can write a word on paper and play with spellings" (9). Rodgers's reference to "spellings" recalls James Weldon Johnson's criticism of dialect poetry, which in turn illustrates the difficulty of developing a complex poetics in which orality is fused with the notion of literature.

Perhaps the best-known critic of Black Arts poetry is Stephen Henderson. In his seminal study, *Understanding the New Black Poetry*,[34] Henderson boldly asserts that the primary references of the new poetry are music and speech.[35] African American poets, he argues, have been largely misinterpreted by both Anglo-American and African American critics because these critics have employed Anglo-American models to analyze the poetry (3). In an attempt to develop a corrective theory to counter the misjudgments of critics of black poetry, Henderson points out that aesthetic values are heavily influenced by a people's cultural and historical experiences, so that their art forms—that is, their perceptions of beauty—are ultimately related to their own view of themselves (4).

Henderson suggests that the misinterpretation of black poetry can be traced to academia. He understands that academic institutions help determine the contours of the discourse on matters pertaining to art. Because these institutions have traditionally been occupied by critics, both black and white, who are largely indifferent to alternatives to Anglo-American standards of art, many black poets whose work is based upon black vernacular culture have been excluded from critical discourse and university classrooms, thereby implying that what has been understood as African American poetry is a gross misrepresentation of the field (3).

Faced with the problem of creating a new critical model, Henderson, like Rodgers, lists eight categories in a section entitled "Black Speech as Poetic

Reference": (1) virtuoso naming and enumerating; (2) jazzy rhythmic effects; (3) virtuoso free-rhyming; (4) hyperbolic imagery; (5) metaphysical imagery; (6) understatement; (7) compressed and cryptic imagery; and (8) worrying the line (33–41). Henderson displays a thorough understanding of the techniques employed in these forms. And though he rarely illustrates how they function in the poetry, it is important to point out that Henderson was writing primarily for an informed audience that knew the poetry firsthand. Consequently, given the seemingly ubiquitous writing workshops across the nation wherein debates concerning politics and poetics were common, Henderson's discussion focuses upon techniques within black vernacular culture generally, so that readers acquainted with black literary discourse could understand the parallels between the former and the latter. Thus, in the category of "compressed and cryptic imagery" (40), Henderson supports his idea by citing a passage from *Invisible Man*.

In his section "Black Music as Poetic Reference" (46), Henderson is even more effective in identifying musical references in the poetry. According to Henderson, the various musical references include:

1. The casual, generalized reference
2. The careful allusion to song titles
3. The quotations from song titles
4. The adaption of song forms
5. The use of tonal memory as poetic structure
6. The use of precise musical notation in the text
7. The use of an assumed emotional response incorporated
8. The musician as subject/poem/history/myth
9. The use of language from the jazz life
10. The poem as "score" or "chart[.]" (47)

In each category, Henderson identifies musical references in the poetry, providing readers with a working study guide. Of course, such works are seldom held in high esteem in academic circles, and Henderson was criticized severely.[36] It is important to bear in mind, however, that his project is primarily (re)constructive. *Understanding the New Black Poetry* provides a critical framework for a national debate among Black Arts writers from various regional, experiential, and theoretical positions, which explains his decision not to conduct conventional criticism wherein theses are supported with textual analyses. Instead, Henderson conducts surveys, identifying kinships between Afro-vernacular and literary discourses. Since *Understanding the New Black Poetry* is an anthology, he had the luxury of referring to poems included in the collection, so that readers could pursue their own line of study: "In Nikki Giovanni's 'Reflections on April 3, 1968' (p. 279) the concluding line is adapted from the title of the Thomas A. Dorsey hymn 'Precious Lord, Take My Hand.' The poet makes this 'Precious Lord—Take Our Hands— Lead / Us On'" (49). While such an observation may seem trivial, Henderson demonstrates that even poems that do not appear to be informed by black song are nonetheless shaped by its contours.

The most important feature of all, though, is the "score" (60). While earlier poets transcribed musical forms onto the page, the poetic score constitutes the most radical formal experiment of the Black Arts movement. The concept of the score, Henderson argues, allows the poet to emphasize performance by deemphasizing the written text. The written poem provides merely a suggestion of what will actually be communicated during the performance: "[There is] a lack of concern with permanence in the Western, Platonic sense of IDEAL FORM. A poem may thus differ from performance to performance just as jazz performances of 'My Favorite Things' would" (61). Though seemingly innocuous given roughly thirty years of hindsight, here Henderson expresses one the basic tenets of the Black Arts Movement, a notion that made the movement one of the most controversial topics in the history of African American criticism—that literature can exist independent of the written page.

Another conceptual component of Henderson's analysis of black poetic form involves his notion of "mascon words" that refer to "a massive concentration of Black experiential energy which powerfully affects the meaning of Black speech, Black song, and Black poetry" (44). He observes that African American cultural history is replete with repetitions of particular words, such as "jook" and "jelly" (44). (The speaker in Destiny's Child's recent song "Bootylicious" boasts of her own jelly for which her interlocutor may not be prepared.[37]) Henderson argues that such words, given their repetition, carry special meanings for African Americans: the title of Faye Adams's song from the fifties, "Shake a Hand, Shake a Hand," is repeated as a line from Gladys Knight's "Friendship Train" in the seventies. The term "roll" provides another example: "'Rock and Roll,' 'Rolling with My Baby,' 'I'm Rolling through an Unfriendly World,' 'Let the Good Times Roll,' 'He sure was rollin' today,' 'Roll 'em Pete,' 'If you can roll your jelly like you roll your dough'" (45). As Henderson says, "roll" refers to a wide range of subjects, including music, labor, sexuality, perseverance, dance, partying, and gambling. The Big Tymers' "Get Your Roll On" illustrates a contemporary example of this phenomenon.[38] Thus, given the kaleidoscopic possibilities of such terms that illustrate the depth of their inscriptions in black vernacular culture, Henderson says, "The poetic potential of all this should be obvious" (45).

But while it is certainly true that readers who are familiar with black lore can appreciate such potentiality, it is also true that those who have little knowledge of black culture may not. Henderson points out that "white critics of Black folk song call these expressions cliches"; however, he "*know*[*s*] that they are mistaken" (45). At issue here is the problem of cultural authority. For Henderson, the major obstacle confronting white critics is race. As "outsider[s]" they cannot understand that contemporary black linguistic practices extend back to slavery (45). Yet it is precisely Henderson's historicism that betrays the breakdown in his cultural nationalist logic. While he rightly objects to misreadings of black art, it is both parochial and self-defeating to assert that only black people can fully understand black poetry (7). Rather than restricting the poets' audience, a revolutionary maneuver would entail an expansion sufficient to render black poetry popular internationally. In other words, it is not race per se but rather the historical forces that construct the mythology of race and thereby mask class exploitation that are responsible for critical myopia; any critic who is willing to question white suzerainty and study black culture (formally or informally) can produce insightful observations about black art.

Although Henderson is the best-known critic of the period, the late Larry Neal was probably the leading theoretician among the poets. Like Rodgers, Neal criticized the superficiality of the movement and correctly observed that poets had ignored the importance of style in African American culture. According to Neal, any claim to a black aesthetic would have to be bolstered by a genuine understanding of vernacular culture.[39]

Like Rodgers, Neal anticipated many of the recent achievements in black critical theory. David Lionel Smith has pointed out the folkloric kinship between Shine, who provides a metaphor for Neal's essay "And Shine Swam On" (7–23), and Gates's *The Signifying Monkey*.[40] Also like Rodgers, Neal rejected much of the wrongheadedness of the movement, such as the idea promoted by Maulana Karenga and Haki Madhubuti that the blues represent subservience and resignation (107). In contrast, Neal sees the blues as a folk literature that, in its ability to preserve the group's history and values, has functioned as a means of cultural resistance: "the blues are basically defiant in their attitude toward life" (108).

But to understand the full implications of the relationship between culture and literature, Neal believed that the African American writer must understand his or her position as a colonized artist. Such an understanding, according to Neal, allows the artist to question the hegemony of dominant forms and to create new ones (25). Though Neal identified himself as a nationalist, his interpretation of nationalism allowed for more diversity than that of his contemporaries. Unlike Madhubuti, Neal recognized the trap of Manichaeism, which leads to a simplistic reversal of privileges, which then constitute nothing more than bourgeois politics in black/brown face.

> We reversed the Manichean dualism that placed the symbolism of blackness on the side of Evil, and whiteness on the side of Good. . . . [This] led to some contradictions, the most important of which was that our nationalism could not exist primarily in contra-distinction to white nationalism. We could never hope to develop a viable concept of self if that concept were purely based on hating. . . . If we made the mistake of constantly addressing scorn and venom to white people, we would fall into the moribund category of the Negro leaders who seemed to be constantly affirming the black man's humanity to white people. (130)

Not surprisingly, then, Neal disagreed with Madhubuti's call for an art that defined African American identity in terms of rats and roaches and insisted upon an oppositional poetics that could stand as excellent art (52).

Neal developed a blues metaphor in his attempt to theorize a revolutionary poetics. According to Neal, black writers have two basic options in this regard. One could excel in the idioms of the dominant culture, achieving a mastery that would allow the artist to redefine the idiom itself. Or the artist could create a completely new form. "Yeah, you can take the other dude's instruments and play like your Uncle Rufus's hog callings," says Neal. "But there is another possibility also: *You can make your own instrument.* And if you can sing through that instrument, you can impose your voice on the world in a heretofore-unthought-of manner" (53). Of course, a third option would involve, as Neal might say, a synthesis of the two approaches. In any case, Neal called upon black poets to reconceptualize the idea of craft by experimenting with music and the sermon: "Listen to James Brown and Malcolm X. We can learn more about what poetry is by listening to the cadences of Malcolm's speeches than from most of Western poetics. Listen to James Brown scream. Ask yourself, then: Have you ever heard a Negro poet sing like that? Of course not, because we have been tied to texts, like most white poets. The text could be destroyed and no one would hurt in the least by it. The key is in the music" (20–21). Here Neal proposes his famous injunction: the destruction of the text. That is, he dismisses the written text and emphasizes the human voice. As such, Neal anticipates hip-hop and spoken word, directing the poetry toward a pre-future poetics[41] in which the human voice becomes an instrument, which transforms the very notion of poetry itself. "Poets," Neal writes, "must learn to sing, dance, and chant their works [and] be a kind of priest" (22).[42]

Yet it is ironic that in his search for models for a black aesthetic in poetry, Neal turns to *Invisible Man*, a *novel*. Citing the critic Albert Murray, Neal calls Ellison's narrative a blues expression par excellence (45). And while I do not disagree, it might have been more useful to readers to apply his concept to black poets. With a cursory glance at the poetry of Sterling Brown, Langston Hughes, and Margaret Walker, Neal illustrates the extent to which all three poets experimented with blues forms. Hughes anticipated Black Arts poetry in his agitprop poetry in the 1930s. Thus, it is not surprising that many poets adopted forms that are more akin to e. e. cummings than poets like Walker or Brown. In this regard, such poets revealed the weaknesses of nationalism. That is, while nationalist intellectuals and artists often claim to represent a distinct culture and tradition, such claims often conceal their own bourgeois visions.[43] Askia Toure and Amiri Baraka have admitted that, at the outset of the movement, they were unfamiliar with the African American literary tradition because, as Henderson points out, privileged histories of literature have consistently rendered the black author invisible.[44]

Moreover, though I agree that song and sermon can provide exciting possibilities for poetry, it should be noted that T. S. Eliot's poetry was instrumental in some African Caribbean poets' discovery of conversational tone that led to an emphasis upon vernacular forms.[45] Thus, Neal repeats the same Manichean maneuver that he opposes. Another problem concerns the issue of the artifact. Like Hughes and Brown had done earlier, Black Arts poets, including Neal, revised the notion of the artifact by recording their work. Yet in his critical work, written a generation before technological breakthroughs produced the compact disc, Neal did not explore the implications of his poetic achievement by theorizing an alternative to the print-versus-live performance dichotomy. That he recorded his work suggests that Neal did not oppose the notion of the artifact as such; he questioned the naturalized hegemony of the page as a specific *type* of artifact because it restricted the poet's artistic possibilities. In any case, it was an unfortunate lapse in vision, because his suggestion that the artifact is marginal to literary discourse perpetuates a logic that deprives literature of a basic function, which is not only to inscribe a group's historical experience from its viewpoint but to *preserve* it as well. James Brown's music, for instance, is only accessible today because it has been recorded.

In neglecting to engage in detailed analyses of the culture, some poets failed to understand *why* black performers are so compelling to audiences. For instance, James Brown's screams, as well as his spellbinding dances, are the result of countless hours of rehearsals. Similarly, as a trained preacher who had been an active participant in hipster culture, Malcolm X understood the oral tradition, particularly the sermon, well enough to politicize it. Some poets did not.

Neal's statement that a poetics can be built upon Malcolm X's sermon technique also raises the complex issue of rhetoric or didacticism as a medium of artistic expression. Henry Louis Gates Jr. articulates the position of many academic critics when, in his dismissal of the poetry of Madhubuti and Baraka, he suggests that rhetoric and poetry are mutually exclusive.[46] However, didacticism does not preclude the possibility of great poetry. As Barbara Harlow argues, "the tendency to dismiss much of Third World poetry derives in fact from the attempted univeral legislation of what is a very local or regionally-based definition poetry, one which, following Aristotle's script in the *Poetics* and the *Rhetoric,* sees in metaphor the essential ingredient of poetic language."[47] Similarly, D. H. Melhem points out that though modernist poets responded to the corruption of language in the early decades of the twentieth century by generating a distrust of abstractions, this perspective, in its extreme manifestation, is itself a kind of dogma.[48]

And yet in their attempt to acknowledge the suffering and beauty of urban black vernacular, some poets created their own dogma. In Sonia Sanchez's "on watching a world series game,"[49] the poet reflects a Manichean perspective in her attack on the popular Boston Red Sox outfielder Carl Yastrzemski. After setting the scene, describing the batter in his preparation for the pitch, Sanchez conducts an analysis of racial politics relative to sports. She astutely suggests that the disproportionate attention focused upon Yaz, as he was popularly called, constitutes a metaphor for white entitlement. She further suggests that, despite baseball's claim to be the nation's favorite sport, Anglo-Americans enjoy exploiting African Americans far more than they enjoy watching baseball. The Red Sox in particular were especially reluctant to hire black players until relatively recently. However, Sanchez ultimately bases her critique of Yastrzemski upon ethnicity, calling him "YASTROOSKI" before moving on to further parody: "ya—fuck—it."

Given Sanchez's considerable talents (her vocal dexterity in her employment of pyrotechnics and rhetorical devices is beyond question), and given the glaring contradictions of race during the late 1960s and early 1970s, one can only imagine the immense popularity of such a poem among black audiences. That Sanchez posits ethnicity as a basis of critique, though, is self-defeating. First, this maneuver fails to account for black complicity in the process of neocolonization. In reducing opposition to a struggle between ethnicities, Sanchez avoids an opportunity to foreground the significance of cultural politics (which was inscribed in such vernacular argot as "oreo cookie"[50]) while deemphasizing identity politics. It is sufficient to point out that the tradition of black conservatism, represented by the likes of Supreme Court Justice Clarence Thomas, extends back to the antebellum period when some slaves chose to fight for the Confederacy. Secondly, Sanchez's attack upon Yastrzemski's ethnicity theoretically preempts the possibility of forming coalitions with other social groups. One of the primary objectives of all social movements is to garner popular support, nationally and internationally. Before his death, Malcolm X envisioned an international coalition wherein "'the majority of white folks will rise up with us.'"[51] Sanchez's chauvinism, which is a logical extension of nationalism,[52] undercuts the basis for potential support from not only sectors of the white working class here in the United States but other disfranchised groups in Africa, Asia, Latin America, the Caribbean and Pacific Islands, Australia, and Europe who could, theoretically at least, identify their struggle with African Americans.[53]

At the same time, given the acerbic response by most academics to Black Arts poetics, I want to underscore the fact that the notion of poetry as performance cannot be dismissed as antipoetry. As the poet and critic Lorenzo Thomas says, "'I think of poetry as performance, and one studies one's craft for the purpose of being able to perform well. . . . [Poetry's] like music in that the practice and the artifact are the same thing. They should get better as time goes on. . . . So the individual poem is not going to change the world unless you believe there are magical sounds which, when uttered, have efficacy in the real world. . . . But then one spends one's time practicing until one is able to produce those sounds effectively.'"[54] The question, as Melhem points out, is not whether rhetoric can be poetic but rather in what manner is it poetic?[55] My argument, which I will develop in chapter 3, is that poetry that approximates the sounds of musicians and/or preachers is best described as incarnations of secular priesthood. In this light, we can understand Black Arts poetry as attempt, with varying degrees of success, to create a resistive, avant-garde poetry that actually approximates the sounds of the preacher and/or musician while simultaneously representing black life from a viewpoint that stimulated audiences to confront the sociopolitical contradictions of their lives.

Similarly, Black Arts criticism demonstrates the potential of colonized groups to create and employ their own critical strategies. Though criticism is often represented in popular culture as an exclusive domain for privileged intellectuals in ivory towers, Black Arts critics exposed the mythology undergirding this view. Not only could an invigorating criticism be produced outside academe; it could also be reconceptualized in form and function. Put differently, Black Arts critics demonstrated the symbiotic relationship between politics and intellectual activity. Having created new art forms to address the harsh realities of the struggle in the streets, writers like Carolyn Rodgers and Larry Neal saw criticism as a medium in which they could lend further assistance to that struggle by examining the ideas that poet/activists employed in cultural production. That such opposition was often restricted to the boundaries of nationalism merely points up the opportunity for a broader, internationalist framework.

3   Elaborations: A Blues Theory
     of African American Poetics

THE CHALLENGE POSED BY Black Arts criticism is formidable indeed. A
generation after the heyday of the movement, critics are still grappling to develop a language in which to discuss the vernacular basis of the poetry and
the political cauldron underlying much of its content. In addition, though
debates over blackness are no longer conducted in terms of who is or is not
an authentic black writer, few critical studies of black poetry have explored
new territory beyond the Manichaeism that Larry Neal identifies in chapter
2. What, then, constitutes a solid basis for new explorations? My response is:
the blues tradition.

Like their counterparts in music, African American resistance poets, that
is, blues poets, engage in expressive acts of cultural resistance. However, since
the phrase "resistance poets" generally refers to colonized poets who are active in resistance movements, I want to emphasize that "resistance poetry"
here refers to a poetry that demonstrates an identification with the repressed
colonized culture by its revision of vernacular forms. Like blues musicians,
blues poets use these forms to counter (mis)representation, describing and
responding to black experiences in styles that challenge conventional definitions of poetry, resisting ideological domination. "Poets of resistance," Barbara Harlow writes, "are attempting to elaborate out of their specific experience new methods and cultural priorities for confronting their historical

situation."[1] Like resistance poets in other colonized areas, blues poets understand that one of the most devastating effects of colonization is the destruction of a people's history and culture.[2] Since many colonized peoples communicated most effectively in oral/aural forms, resistance poets understand that a poetics based upon music can be an effective tool in assisting readers to kill the colonizer within their own psyches.[3] The internal death allows poets and audiences to participate in collective resistance against misrepresentation.

My selection of blues music as a metaphor for a critical model of African American poetry represents my attempt to examine black poetic form without a vulgar formalism or a nationalist trap such as Manichaeism. Though blues music (as distinct from having the blues, that is, feelings of sadness)[4] is concerned with the specific experiences of African Americans, it rejects simplistic binary oppositions. Instead, blues music expresses an urge for expansion, that is, a preference for the word "and." Thus, it is an excellent model for an oppositional criticism whose recognition of marginalization moves the critical procedure beyond nationalism to *inter*nationalism. In this context, racism does not constitute colonization itself but rather a specific type. Hence, internationalism allows the critic to acknowledge the value of other traditions of resistance and thereby participate in a universal struggle for liberation.

Blues Music as Cultural Network

Long before anonymous black bards created the poetry and music that people would eventually call the blues, other black musicians suffered the tragic loss of their drums, which were essential to African discursive modes. The story of the blues tradition, beginning with what W. E. B. Du Bois called the sorrow songs, narrates the subsequent dialectical interchanges between colonizer and colonized, theft, exploitation, and (re)creation in a drama without closure. The blues, Ralph Ellison might say, were in the cards as soon as the first slave ship arrived in 1619. Nearly four hundred years later in the mid-1980s, I sat in a funky dive and listened to Koko Taylor express her determination to "pitch a wang dang doodle all night long." Taylor's line sums up the resiliency and determination to survive that black peasants displayed in the rural South before and after the Civil War. On the surface, the line bears little relation to a resistive effort of any type. Upon further reflection, though, it becomes evident that this single line inscribes the historical function of the black oral tradition. The onomatopoeia recalls the use of seemingly meaningless sound as codes to convey feelings and ideas. The apparently innocuous denotation of the phrase (to throw a party) evokes ironically the painful working conditions in the plantation South and urban North in that it reflects the people's determination to create pleasure in a world designed to deny such a pursuit. Such is the stuff of the blues.

Taylor's song constitutes one vector of the blues impulse. Abbey Lincoln's work represents another. In "Retribution,"[5] she reflects a politicized consciousness, calling for retributive action commensurate with the contributions that blacks have made to American society. In so doing, she anticipates contemporary calls for reparations for slavery by summing up the exploitive nature of colonization while suggesting radical change as a dialectical response. Thus, albeit in contrasting modalities, both songs exemplify the capacity for resistance in the blues tradition, that is, the ability to express feelings of candor in an idiom especially suited to the sensibilities of African Americans.[6]

Analytical discussions of the blues often include definitions of the blues, though the very description of the blues is difficult because the word can refer to a wide range of different things: "emotion, a technique, a musical form, and a song lyric."[7] The word "blues," in its original sense, seems to have come from the despondent mood associated with having a fit of "blue devils" that anyone could experience. The phrase "blue devils" was employed in Elizabethan England,[8] and during the nineteenth century, people such as Lord Byron, Washington Irving, and Thomas Jefferson used the words "blues" and "blue devils" in their writings (Tracy 59).

Many standard definitions of blues music begin by referring to an aab pattern in which twelve bars are divided into four sections that consist of three lines. The first line is repeated (often with some variation), and the last line rhymes with the first. In addition, there are other stanzaic patterns common in blues songs, including aaa, aaab, ab, and ab with a refrain.

However, blues music cannot be described adequately by stanzaic patterns alone. Much of the emotional force of the music comes from its instrumentation (Murray 82). The importance of understanding blues songs as lyrical expressions notwithstanding, a deeper significance of the music lies in its propensity for synthesis. As an amorphous form, the blues are characterized by both subsumption and infusion. In fact, the blues are themselves products of hybridization. In addition to the ballads' capacity to resolve contradictions (God/Devil, bad/good),[9] which stemmed from the spirituals, the blues absorbed other forms, including "fables, metaphors, and melodies. Field hollers supplied vocal techniques and tonality. More than likely the 'blue notes' had their origins in the arhoolies. Work songs supplied antiphony, cross-rhythms, and important thematic material."[10] Thus, blues music is a model of dynamism and creolization, constantly assuming new shapes and forms while preserving its distinctiveness.

Herein lies the special nature of the blues idiom. While the blues performer may sing songs from various genres, blues music maintains an ability to render a particular configuration of sound that listeners recognize as the blues. Blues music constitutes a metastyle, that is, a style of styles. Although it includes songs performed according to the stanzaic patterns listed above, my conceptualization of the music encompasses nearly the entire black oral/aural tradition, ranging from earlier forms such as ballads and arhoolies to jazz and rhythm and blues. My inclusion of jazz as a blues expression is not an arbitrary maneuver. As I will demonstrate later, the blues comprise the very basis of jazz. But before I discuss the relationship between blues and jazz, I would like to discuss the relationship of the blues to its forerunners.

During slavery, the aural component of the black oral tradition was manifested most often in spirituals. But though the spirituals preceded the blues, their contribution to the blues was not musical. Instead, spirituals preserved the oral tradition, and they provide important clues to blues music's psychology and creative process. For instance, though there were thematic similarities, spirituals differed according to region, just as Mississippi Delta blues differs from Texas blues.

More importantly, spirituals, like other antebellum forms, supplied the blues with source material for formal revision. Jon Michael Spenser points out that blues artists not only revised ballads like "John Henry"; they also revised such spirituals as "Trouble in Mind," "Sometimes I Feel Like a Motherless Child," and, especially, "Nobody Knows the Trouble I've Seen."[11] Whereas sacred singers sang,

Nobody knows the trouble I've seen,
Nobody knows my sorrow.
Nobody knows the trouble I've seen,
Glory Hallelujah!

blues singers sang about misfortunes with women. In "Pleading Blues," Eurreal Montgomery sang about a no-good woman and concluded with the line: "Nobody knows but the good Lord and me." Red Nelson, in "Crying Mother Blues," sang, "Nobody knows my troubles but myself and the good Lord," and in 1939 Jimmy Rushing, who performed with the Count Basie Orchestra, sang the same line but substituted "baby" for "Lord."[12]

Other blues songs, such as Sippie Wallace's "Go Down Sunshine," "Shorty George," and "Section Hand Blues," were based upon well-known work songs (Barlow 143). Note the absence of repetition that informs the conventional blues in "Section Hand Blues":

> If my captain ask for me,
> Tell him Abe Lincoln set us free,
> Ain't no hammer on this road,
> Gonna kill poor me.
> This ole hammer killed John Henry,
> But this hammer ain't gonna kill me.
> I'm headin' for my shack,
> With my shovel on my back,
> Although money's what I lack,
> I'm goin home.[13]

The usual practice of separating blues and jazz is misleading because it denies the historical basis of jazz.[14] Jazz musicians were responsible for establishing the twelve-bar blues as a standard form (Barlow 40). Bessie Smith fired her pianist to hire Fletcher Henderson. Early New Orleans musicians did not often make distinctions between the two words (186). Buddy Bolden, the first great jazz virtuoso, was popular largely because of his band's blues performances. Dude Botley, for instance, does not mention the word "jazz" in his recollection of Bolden's music:

> For a while [the music] sounds like the blues, then like a hymn. I cannot make out the tune, but after a while I catch on. He is *mixing* up the blues with the hymns. He plays the blues *real* sad and the hymn sadder than the blues and then the blues sadder than the hymn. . . . I close my eyes, and *when he blows the blues I picture Lincoln Park with all them sinners and whores shaking and belly rubbing. Then, as he blows the hymn, I picture my mother's church on Sunday, and everybody humming with the choir.* The picture in my mind kept changing with the music as he blew. It sounded like a battle between the Good Lord and the Devil. Something tells me to listen and see who wins. If he stop on the blues, the Devil wins.[15]

And Jelly Roll Morton, who, according to Albert Murray, "seems to have been ragging, stomping, jazzing, and riffing everything within earshot at least as early as 1900" (86), implies that Bolden played dance music when he says, "'I remember we'd be hanging around some corner, wouldn't know that there was going to be a dance out at Lincoln Park. Then we'd hear old Buddy's trumpet coming on and we'd all start. Any time it was quiet at night at Lincoln Park because maybe the affair hadn't been so well publicized, Buddy Bolden would publicize it! He'd turn his trumpet around toward the city and blow his *blues,* calling his children home, as he used to say'" (qtd. in Murray 144). Finally, the saxophonist Buster Smith, who played in Benny Moten's band in Kansas City, recalls jazz in Dallas in the 1920s: "'We usually called our music barrelhouse or gutbucket. . . . We didn't use the word jazz very often'" (qtd. in Barlow 133). Smith's statement suggests that the distinction between the two terms did not come from the musicians themselves. It also provides a basis for understanding why instrumentalists have become the dominant stylists of blues music. Kansas City bands of the 1930s produced a fusion of blues and jazz. Moten's band, which became Count Basie's after Moten died in 1935, featured the legendary saxophonist Lester Young and the blues singer Jimmy Rushing. The largely unfettered collaborations between blues singers and jazz musicians, in clubs and late jam sessions, created a new riffing style that allowed more solo space and emphasized the vocal techniques of blues singers: "Effects such as vibrato, pitch variation, tremolo, and slurring and sliding notes were all commonplace among the city's horn players" (Barlow 247). Basie's blues-oriented innovations prefigured the bebop of the 1940s.

The Kansas City fusion of blues and jazz suggests that jazz is an urban manifestation of the blues idiom, that is, a more sophisticated elaboration of blues music. As Tracy says, "From the beginning of jazz performing, it has been obvious that the jazz musician plays the blues differently from the blues musician. The jazz musician has a tendency to be more sophisticated, to improvise in a more complex manner and at greater length, and to de-emphasize the words of songs and subordinate them to instrumental expressiveness and variations, though the jazz musician often imitates the human voice" (245). Tracy's statement suggests that the terms "blues" and "jazz" are useful in acknowledging varying levels of musical complexity in the blues. However, if we can accept my description of blues music as a dynamic form, the passage does not contradict my thesis that jazz is an expression of the blues idiom. Eric Hobsbawm, echoing Charlie Parker's statement about the relationship between jazz and blues, argues: "'The blues is not a style or phase of jazz, but its heart.'"[16]

The personal nature of blues music allows for the expression of a group experience to be mediated through individuals. Consequently, critics have mistakenly assumed that blues songs are autobiographical. Howard Odum and Guy Johnson, writing in the 1920s, describe the blues as "'the wail of the despondent Negro'" (qtd. in Tracy 197). Roughly thirty years later, Ralph Ellison echoed Odum and Johnson, stating that the blues are "an autobiographical chronicle of personal catastrophe expressed lyrically."[17] However, the autobiographical mode often functions as an artistic device that maximizes the effectiveness of the blues singer's narrative. As secular priests, blues singers are firmly committed to their audiences. Though they may be relatively quiet in private life, blues singers present public selves, that is, personas that perform in public. B. B. King explains: "'I've seen many people hurt, homes broken, people killed . . . so I sing about it'" (qtd. in Tracy 101). And the former blues artist Reverend Rubin Lacy recalls that his composition "Mississippi Jailhouse Groan" was not inspired by his own experience in prison: "'Sometimes I'd propose [lyrics] as [if] it happened to me in order to hit somebody else, 'cause everything that happened to one person has at some time or other happened to another one. If not, it will.'"[18] Blues songs are therefore less lyrical autobiographies than, as Houston Baker says, "phylogenetic recapitulation[s] . . . of species experience."[19]

In its ability to express the concerns of the community, the blues function as a cultural matrix. As Baker observes, "A matrix is a womb, a network, a fossil-bearing rock . . . a point of ceaseless input and output, a web of intersecting, crisscrossing impulses always in productive transit."[20] I agree with Baker's idea, but the word "matrix" suggests a womb or origins. The blues are undoubtedly both "womb" and "origins," in relation to postbellum forms, yet the term "matrix" denies the historical importance of spirituals, ballads, and other antebellum forms.

Consequently, I have selected the phrase "blues network" to describe blues music's central position in African American vernacular culture. As a trope for critical inquiry in black poetry, the blues network functions as a junction, a (super)conductor, intersecting classes, cultures, and continents. To be privy to a performance of the blues network is to claim witness to a dialogue of creative recipes that culminates in a veritable gumbo of art. Here the critical observer discovers the quintessence of collaboration: Baptist preachers and rappers of the profane, spiritual and gospel singers alongside the blues, and jazz virtuosos listening for a riff.

My conception of a blues network follows the examples provided by black musicians themselves. Like hip-hop crews today, "there were numerous informal networks, 'extended families,' or 'schools' of blues musicians" (40). Blues "schools" or networks usually depended on the prominence of a local musician who, in turn, influenced other (often younger) musicians. In the Mississippi Delta blues, for example, a blues network revolved around Charley Patton.

Patton recorded fifty titles, including thirty-five blues, ten religious songs, three ballads, and two ragtime songs. The son of a lay preacher who received guitar lessons from members of the Chatmon family, then in its third generation of performing music, Patton was heir to a rich oral tradition (37), which preserved an African approach to musicianship involving the merging of voice and instrument.[21] Patton could simulate the human voice on his guitar, and he often resorted to melisma, experimenting with his own voice. Consequently, many of his lyrics are unintelligible. Robert Palmer observes:

> Patton often seemed to alter the stresses of conventional speech for purely musical ends. In his recording of "Pony Blues," for example, he stretches certain syllables and inserts split-second pauses between words in order to achieve a desired rhythmic effect. "Come a sto-orm last night and to-o-re the [pause] wire down," he sings, stretching the "down" into the next measure and . . . alternately constricting and relaxing his throat muscles. . . . These vocal techniques . . . are basic attributes of superior Delta blues singing.[22]

Patton's direct influence on the blues can be seen in the music of three men who played with him—Willie Brown (who was married to Josie Bush, one of the few women country blues singers), Tommy Johnson, and Son House.

Johnson became a great showman, playing his guitar behind his back and head, like Patton. The Delta blues performer Houston Stackhouse observes: "'He'd kick the guitar, flip it, turn it back of his head and be playin' it, then he'd get straddled over it like he was ridin' a mule; pick it that way. . . . People loved to see that.'"[23] Brown's reputation rests largely upon his guitar playing. Though Brown sang the blues, younger guitarists were drawn to his approach to the guitar, which involved new instrumental interpretations of the blues. But while Brown had produced innovations in blues rhythms, Son House was one of the first blues musicians to master the bottleneck technique of guitar playing, which improved upon the knife-blade technique that musicians had employed to produce a whining sound.

Drawing from traditional African aesthetic theories, the merging of voice and instrument became one of the hallmarks of black music. One recalls the scat singing of Louis Armstrong and Ella Fitzgerald as well as the tongue-twisting gymnastics of the rap artist Busta Rhymes. Similarly, though she did not scat, Billie Holiday described her singing as synonymous with horn blowing. Today, the singer Dee Dee Bridgewater and the hip-hop musician Scratch continue to experiment with the voice/instrument approach. On her rendition of Horace Silver's composition "Doodlin," Bridgewater improvises a wordless solo that approximates the sound of a trombone, and on "Don't

See Us," the beatboxer Scratch captures the scratching sounds of a DJ so fully that MC Black Thought refers to him as a "human turntablist."[24]

Conversely, blues instrumentalists, beginning with Buddy Bolden, have continued the blues whine or cry. In the 1960s, musicians such as John Coltrane, Ornette Coleman, Cecil Taylor, and Eric Dolphy attempted to create a new jazz sound. Critics attacked it as antijazz, but Dolphy disagreed. "'This human thing in instrumental playing,'" said Dolphy, "'has to do with trying to get as much human warmth and feeling into my work as I can. I want to say more on my horn than I ever could in ordinary speech.'"[25] Dolphy's account of his approach recalls Stuart Hall's contention that within the deep grooves of orality in black music lie alternative styles of life that challenge the naturalization of Herrenvolk democracy.[26]

Of course, all cultures are oral in the literal sense of the term, since speech and song are ubiquitous among human beings. My use of the phrase "oral culture" refers to the great emphasis that is placed upon speech and/or song as mediums of communication. Though all cultures use verbal communication, some rely more on oral forms to convey ideas.[27] While print-oriented cultures use writing to store information, other cultures tend to communicate via performance or demonstration. As Ben Sidran says, "he *becomes* the information."[28]

The propensity for the physical assimilation of sound suggests the real significance of the voice/instrument approach. Deprived of conventional skills developed in hegemonic institutions, blues singers expressed their ideas in a medium of sound that functioned as aural calligraphy.[29] Though literal content is certainly important, it is also clear, as Richard Bauman points out, that people respond to sounds that escape denotation: "in artistic performances of this kind, there is something going on in the communicative interchange which says to the auditor, 'interpret what I say in some special sense; do not take it to mean what the words alone, taken literally, would convey.'"[30]

Bauman's comment suggests that vocal techniques such as blue notes in music and half-cry chants in sermons should be understood not only as examples of technical virtuosity but also as sonic script that lends spiritual resonance to the audience. Though blues lyrics describe the experiences of the community, the blues performer's success is based upon his or her ability to produce sounds that *evoke* the experiences of the community. As Jeff Todd Titon argues while quoting the blues singer Baby Doo Caston, "'Blues is a sound. . . . it's a feeling that a sound would put you into.' A downhome blues song locates downhome as a feeling in the listener's mental landscape. . . . In the city, downhome blues . . . remind listeners of the feeling of life down home."[31] Similarly, John Coltrane has said, "'I recognize an individual when I see his contribution; and when I know a man's sound, well, to me that's him, that's the man.'"[32]

The statements by Caston and Coltrane attest to the importance of sound as well as the personal nature of the blues tradition that allows for infinite variations. Mutt Carey's account of his first experience hearing Louis Armstrong exemplifies this quality: "'I let Louis sit in my chair. Now at that time I was the 'Blues King' of New Orleans, and when Louis played that day he played more blues than I ever heard in my life. It never did strike my mind that blues could be interpreted so many different ways. Every time he played a chorus, it was different and you knew it was a blues. Yes, it was all blues'" (qtd. in Barlow 191). Carey's description of Armstrong's performance illustrates the capacity for diversity in the collective experience of blues music.

Thus, blues music is an omnidemocratic form. Though it is a response to racist conditions and attitudes, it does not lend itself well to knee-jerk reactions of chauvinism. Blues music describes conditions that are specific to African Americans, but it is performed by people of other cultural groups as well. In this way, the blues idiom constitutes an American form of national liberation in song and poetry.

Blues Music as Resistance

    Q. What did God make you for?
    A. To make a crop.
    Q. What is the meaning of "Thou shalt not commit adultery"?
    A. To serve our heavenly Father, and our earthly master, obey our overseer, and not steal anything.[33]

This catechism demonstrates the slaveholders' attempt to dehumanize slaves and render them totally subservient. Though slaves suffered horrible physical hardships, their quest for self-definition was even more difficult. In the attempt to remove any viable means of developing an Africanist sense of agency, slave masters banned African drums and suggested that freedom was as remote as Africa. But the majority of the slaves never believed it. In "Oh Freedom," the slaves sang,

    Oh Freedom! Oh Freedom!
    Oh Freedom, I love thee!

And before I'll be a slave,
I'll be buried in my grave,
And go home to my Lord and be free.

Other songs, such as "No More Auction Block for Me" and "Go Down, Moses," also inscribed the desire for liberation. Yet most spirituals are not direct expressions of their hatred of slavery. At times, slaves used songs as codes, as did Harriet Tubman in participating in the Underground Railroad:

You might be Carroll from Carrolton
Arrive here night afo' Lawd make creation
But you can't keep the World from movering around
And not turn her back from the gaining ground.[34]

While these lyrics seem relatively innocuous, the words "not turn her" suggest a sly allusion to Nat Turner. Most often, though, "slave music," as Lawrence W. Levine argues, "presented the slave with a potential outlet for his individual feelings even while it continually drew him back into the communal presence and permitted him the comfort of basking in the warmth of the shared assumptions of those around him" (33).

Similarly, most blues songs are not directly political. This is not to suggest that the music is devoid of politics, however. As Angela Davis argues, "social protest can never be made the exclusive or limiting function of art. . . . In the absence of a popular mass movement, [art] can only encourage a critical attitude."[35] The political significance of blues music stems largely from its capacity for communicating certain feelings and ideas as well as its inscription of African American style. As Sidney Finkelstein points out, the ear apprehends the configuration of certain sounds as human images that describe a people's experience in a society.[36] And as the blues critic Samuel Charters argues, "'Whatever else the blues was it was a language, a rich, vital, expressive language that stripped away the misconception that the black society in the United States was simply a poor, discouraged version of the white. It was impossible not to hear the differences.'"[37]

Disfranchised and illiterate because of the economics of slavery, African American communities (re)constructed African-derived aesthetics that led to the development of various expressive forms. Recall the fact that not only Nat Turner but Martin Luther King Jr. and Malcolm X were preachers. Similarly, the blues musician's pervasive influence in his or her community stems from his or her role as a secular priest.[38] It is important to clarify that I am not referring to an adherence to any set of organized philosophical principles, even though James Cone has described the blues idiom as secular spirituals.[39] I am referring to the musicians' exalted position in working-class African American communities, which is based upon their ability to testify to the truths of the people's experiences. Again, this performative style, as Ben Sidran points out, is prefigured in the spirituals, wherein the "preacher took the role of lead singer[;] the group actionality was generated by the vocal and rhythmic response of the congregation . . . and the musical-religious ritual became the important single experience in the daily life of the slave, much as it had been in pre-slavery Africa."[40] After the overthrow of Reconstruction, however, the glaring contradictions between the brutal realities of sharecropping and the angelic images of the hereafter became too explosive to be housed inside the church, so the blues packed a box lunch, as it were, and left. In the new expressive form, references to everyday life displaced the theology of the spirituals; hence, the original designation of the blues as the "reals" (Barlow 326).

The combination of the church's failure to address important social issues and blues artists' creative responses to the people's experiences lent blues musicians a measure of leadership in the black community. "The off-duty blues musician," according to Murray, "tends to remain in character much as does the Minister of the Gospel, and as he makes the rounds he also receives a special deference from the Saturday Night Revelers equivalent to that given off-duty ministers by Sunday Morning Worshippers" (230). Gene Gilmore's "The Natchez Fire" provides a case in point. Although a secular song, "The Natchez Fire" functioned as a eulogy for two hundred victims of a fire in Natchez, Mississippi, in April 1940: "'Lord, I know, I know how you Natchez people feel today; / some of them thinking of the fire that took their children's life away.'"[41]

Many blues musicians were from religious backgrounds, and an equal number became preachers either before or after their experiences as blues musicians. But most importantly, as Barlow observes, many musicians describe their performances as religious experiences. For instance, the New Orleans guitarist and banjo player Danny Barker describes Bessie Smith's effect on her audience: "'She could bring about mass hypnotism. When she was performing you could hear a pin drop. . . . When you went to see Bessie . . . if you had any church background, like people who came from the South, like I did, you would recognize a similarity between what she was doing and what those preachers and evangelists from there did, and how they moved people. . . . Bessie did the same thing on stage'" (qtd. in Barlow 170–71). Similarly, we are told, Buddy Bolden played his cornet in a manner that sounded "'just like you were in church'" (189). And though their music became much more complex, modern jazz musicians maintained this perception of their music. The pianist Thelonius Monk, for instance, was known among jazz enthusiasts as the High Priest, and the trumpeter Dizzy Gillespie says, "The message of our music runs the same way as the message of religion."[42] Hence, Coltrane's description of his composition *A Love Supreme* as a sort of prayer.[43]

In their roles as secular priests, blues musicians reflect and refract an African American sensibility. Yet blues music, as Albert Murray argues, "is a by-product . . . of all cultural elements that brought that sensibility into being in the first place."[44] Blues music exemplifies a process of creolization that creates an omni-American form. Yet the artistic forms that have been shaped by the blues, as well as the styles of life reflected therein, have been consistently marginalized by the dominant institutions of this society. Such antipathy toward blues styles not only constitutes an exclusion of working-class black people per se; it represents nothing less than an attempt to confine conceptualizations of Americana within the pale scope of whiteness, a determined refusal to accept the reality that the West is now African, Indian, Latino, and Asian. As Miles Davis says, "I don't see why our music can't be given the respect of European classical music. Beethoven's been dead all these years and they're still talking about him, teaching him, and playing his music. Why ain't they talking about Bird, or Trane, or Monk, or Duke, or Count, or Fletcher Henderson, or Louis Armstrong like they're talking about Beethoven? . . . *We're all Americans now,* and sooner or later whites are going to have to deal with all the great things that black people have done here."[45] Davis does not advocate a reductive position of ignoring Beethoven's music. Instead, he favors teaching Beethoven *and* blues music.

Part of the resistive challenge in the blues idiom involves its rejection of traditional Christian views toward the body. Rather than associating sensuality with sin, the eroticism of Afro-vernacular dance can be interpreted as an enchanting celebration of the human life cycle wherein physical pleasure is vital to procreation itself. Similarly, blues music deals in ritual and incantation. The desired effect conjoins flesh and spirit and compels physical movement. As the pianist James P. Johnson says, "'Man, if they ain't patting their feet, you ain't swinging and ain't nothing happening'" (qtd. in Murray, *Stomping* 244).

As a secular priest, the blues musician's capacity to stimulate emotional rejuvenation helps to explain one of the most misunderstood aspects of the blues. While the conventional view of the blues connotes sadness, the music, even in the most ostensibly sad songs, arouses pleasure in its audiences. This is possible because blues music emphasizes passion and desire in its dealings with everyday reality, which includes the world of the flesh, so that the central aim of the music is to stimulate sensations. "Blues music," Murray writes, "almost always induces dance movement that is the direct opposite of resignation" (45). The soothing feelings the music generates allow audiences to affirm their own humanity by reaffirming the peoples' values and preserving their cultural memories in a medium of sound. Since blues music tends to locate specific, corresponding geographies in the listeners' mental landscape, it can evoke the feeling of the lifestyle that is remembered.[46]

Sometimes the blues idiom is overtly political. The Afrocentricity of Archie Shepp's "The Magic of Juju" and Don Pullen's pensive "Suite (Sweet) Malcom (Part 1: Memories and Gunshots)" serve as two examples of conscious politicization in jazz. More recently, the blues singer Willie King has reflected his commitment to social change in Pickens County, Alabama, on his album entitled *Freedom Creek Blues*. In contemporary forms of black music, such musicians and/or groups as KRS-One, Public Enemy, Eve, Dead Prez, Common, Mos Def, Tupac Shakur, The Coup, Erykah Badu, Jill Scott, and India Arie have, in varying degrees, engaged in overt social protest. During the era of the classic blues, Bessie Smith recorded "Poor Man's Blues," wherein she addresses class politics. This song stands as one of the most noteworthy artworks in American history. And while her biographer Chris Albertson has suggested that Smith "'had no interest in politics,'"[47] her masterpiece of social criticism demonstrates that her work was far more advanced politically than that of many Harlem Renaissance writers. If we recall Alain Locke's contention in chapter 2 that most black writers hold relatively conservative views on class issues but support radical change on racial issues,[48] Smith's perspicacity becomes crystal clear:

> Poor man fought all the battles, poor man would fight again today,
> Poor man fought all the battles, poor man would fight again today,
> He would do anything you ask him in the name of the U.S.A.
> Now the war is over, poor man must live the same as you,
> Now the war is over, poor man must live the same as you,
> If it wasn't for the poor man, Mr. Rich man what would you do?[49]

Smith adroitly avoids what Frantz Fanon calls the "pitfalls of national consciousness" by opting not to romanticize workers.[50] Instead, she emphasizes their exploitation, suggesting that their lack of an economic base renders them subject to the ideas created within the capitalist superstructure.

Most often, though, blues songs are not overtly political, and yet the music is nonetheless an art of confrontation. As a phylogenetic form, blues lyrics often reflect both the ex-slave's living conditions and his or her emotional responses to them: "'Got the blues, but too damn mean to cry.'"[51] Or: "'Ought's a ought, figger's a figger / All for the white man, none for the nigger.'"[52] Rough-and-tumble toughness in the face of adversity compels the persona to act—even if this means leaving: "'I'd rather drink muddy water, sleep in a hollow log / Dan to stay in dis town, treated like a dirty dog.'"[53] Since the persona is usually the victim of a bad situation, the decision to leave and his consequent freedom represent victory over the miscreant in question. And while this may appear superficially as resignation, the primary point of singing about mistreatment is usually to expose the contradictions of the abuser— whether he or she is a lover, friend, or authority figure:[54]

Lord, they accused me of murder, murder, murder,
I haven't harmed a man,
Ohh, they accused me of murder
And I have't harmed a man.
Oh, they accused me of forgery,
And I—I can't even write my name,
Lord, they accused me of forgery

I can't even write my name.[55]

The ability to express contradictions in blues music stems from an Afro-vernacular worldview that often opposes rigid categorization. In the black lexicon, the term "bad" can also mean good. Caught in a philosophical framework that restricted one's consciousness to either meekness (Jesus) or recalcitrance (the Devil), many working-class blacks have chosen (and continue to choose) the latter because the former has often led directly into a puritannical constriction. As Peetie Wheatstraw puts it, "They say we are the Lord's children, I don't say that ain't true / But if we are the same like each other, ooh, well, why do they treat me like they do?"[56] Hence, it is not surprising that the church's condemnation of the blues as the Devil's music seems only to have intensified audiences' attraction to it. In fact, Wheatstraw, one of the most popular blues musicians in his era, described himself as the Devil's Son-in-Law, the High Sheriff from Hell.

The propensity for contradictions in blues lyrics can also lead to a heightened sense of social consciousness expressed in humorous self-mockery and irony. Big Bill Broonzy, for instance, sang: "Yeah, poor me's down so low, baby, Big Bill is lookin' up at down."[57] Broonzy's wit is sharp, his insight profound. The persona occupies an ontological space for which there exists no language. How, indeed, does one look up at down? The phrase illustrates, in microcosm, the surreality of race. Broonzy unmasks it, evaporating the fog hovering over the mythology of race so that readers can discern the peculiar underbelly of American class politics.

Similarly, blues women used blues lyrics to address mistreatment by black men. When men sang such lyrics as, "If you got a little woman, don't never hit her too hard / She'll swell up like doughnut when you throw it in the lard,"[58] women like Victoria Spivey responded with songs like "Bloodhound Blues": "Well, I poisoned my man, I put it in his drinking cup, / Well, I poisoned my man, I put it in his drinking cup, / Well, it's easy to go to jail, but lawd, they sent me up."[59] "Bloodhound Blues" anticipates the intensity of Eve's "Love Is Blind,"[60] wherein the persona engages in a sort of fictional enactment of Lincoln's "Retribution" by killing her dead friend's lover. Similarly, TLC's "No Scrubs,"[61] which signifies on would-be players, is a rejoinder to Lizzie Miles's "I Hate a Man Like You," wherein the persona criticizes her man's hypocrisy:

> I hate a man like you, don't like the things you do,
> When I met you, I thought you was right,
> You married me and stayed out the first night.
> Just like a woman you're always carrying tales,
> Trying to make trouble, wanna get me in jail,
> Then you can't find no one to go my bail.
> Lawd, I hate a man like you.[62]

By signifying on male opportunists, blues women attempted to discourage mistreatment while simultaneously "communicat[ing] to women listeners that they were members of a sisterhood that did not have to tolerate mistreatment."[63] In this respect, as Angela Davis points out, blues women anticipated the feminist movement of the 1970s by demonstrating that the "'personal *is* political.'"[64] Ida Cox's title "Wild Women Don't Have the Blues" underscores the oppositional politics underlying such songs. Ma Rainey even questioned heterosexuality as a naturalized practice in "Prove It on Me Blues,"[65] wherein she boldly affirms the right to engage in lesbian relationships. As Davis argues, much of the material that public intellectuals use to conceptualize black feminism "tends to exclude ideas produced by and within poor and working-class communities, where women historically have not had the means or access to publish written texts."[66]

Though Davis refers directly to blues women, her comment has implications for studies of vernacular cultures generally. Just as such texts as Mos Def's "Mathematics" expose the contradictions of postmodern America, so blues music functions, as it were, as a people's literature. The raucous nature of the blues, that is, its bout-it, bout-it[67] rowdiness and utter refusal to genuflect, lies at the core of the music. The determination to seek to improve conditions in spite of rigid social barriers can be interpreted in political terms as a blues-inflected struggle for meaningful change.

Kinds of Blues

In designating the blues network as a trope for African American poetry, I am suggesting that black poets approximate the role of the blues musician in several respects. The adulation that is bestowed upon blues poets closely resembles that which is accorded blues musicians. The best poetic performances elicit vocal responses and/or physical movements not unlike Sunday congregations. Also, though it is not common for blues poets to mock or parody vernacular forms, like blues musicians they do incorporate vernacular forms into their poetry. Moreover, some poets employ paralinguistic techniques that are either reproductions of blues techniques or approximations of them, such as singing, scatting, screaming, melisma, chanting, and voice inflection.

Blues poets also engage in cultural syncretism by interpreting the Western concept of literature within the context of African American vernacular culture, thereby extending both traditions while simultaneously redefining notions of poetry and artifact. But when professional critics attack or ignore blues poets because their forms illustrate an alternative set of aesthetic values, they reify Anglo-American privilege by suggesting that one cultural perspective is inherently more valuable than another.

At the same time, it is important to note that, also like blues music, there is not a monolithic approach to the poetry. Most blues poets write poems that should be read aloud, and all demonstrate some type of formal relationship to black vernacular culture. Yet they do so differently. Some poets transcribe oral forms almost directly onto the page, while others attempt to fuse vernacular forms with literary conventions, and others employ voice/instrument technique. Yet even blues poets themselves do not always write blues poems. Consequently, the question for critics is: what kind of blues poem is it?

I have selected three blues-related terms as metaphors that describe how vernacular culture informs African American poetry. These tropes do not signify rigid categories (some poets use a combination of approaches), but they do offer critical tools that give readers new perspectives about black poetic forms. They are: riffing and the changing same; epistrophy, or the performance of cultural (re)memory; and cutting sessions, or the incarnation of secular priesthood.

Riffing and the Changing Same

Before blues singers developed the twelve-bar, aab structure, many blues songs, like the earlier hollers and shouts, were formed by the repetition of a single line. In jazz, the repeated phrase is called a riff. Riffing is also present in the black church tradition. Mahalia Jackson, who was as popular among blues enthusiasts as among churchgoers (despite her well-known refusal to sing blues lyrics), employs the riff extensively in her song "How I Got Over,"[68] repeating the phrase "I feel like shoutin'" with different stresses and tonal inflections. The riff is also present in the call and response of the black sermon:

> "Solo-call: On the mountain.
> Congregation: I couldn't hear nobody pray.
> Solo: In the valley.
> Riff: Couldn't hear nobody.
> Solo: On my kneehees.
> Riff: Couldn't hear nobody.
> Solo: With my Jesus.
> Riff: Couldn't hear nobody.
> Solo: Oh, Lord.
> Riff: I couldn't hear nobody.
> Solo: Oh, Lordahawd!!!
> Riff: Couldn't hear nobody pray.
> Everybody: Way down yonder by myself
>   I couldn't hear nobody pray." (qtd. in Murray 27–30)

While there are sometimes subtle changes in the riff, the repeated phrase can be recognized clearly.

One clue to how riffing functions as a trope can be observed in vernacular culture. On a tune entitled "Blue Monk/Stormy Monday,"[69] the Dirty Dozen Brass Band Band uses Thelonius Monk's tune "Blue Monk" and the popular blues song "Stormy Monday" as bases for "improvising new melodies over old rhythms."[70] The originality of "Blue Monk/Stormy Monday" stems largely from the band's ability to perform the two pieces simultaneously within the context of the New Orleans marching-band tradition. What is most distinctive about this style of performance is the striking similarity between the antecedent tunes and the revised performance.

As a trope, then, riffing refers to a kind of mimetic pastiche. The revisionary text is, in form, a thinly disguised version of another expressive act or form. In other words, creative artists who riff tropologically create near-replicas of aural/oral forms. Recall Murray's statement that riffing includes the repetition of "stock phrases" (96). Thus, the saxophonist John Handy's "If We Only Knew" can be viewed as a riff on John Coltrane's "Spiritual," since he repeats many of Coltrane's phrases.[71] Similarly, Baraka points out that "many bop 'originals' were really rephrased versions of popular songs like *Indiana, I Got Rhythm, Honeysuckle Rose, Cherokee,* etc."[72]

Such formal relationships are also common in the tradition of black song. Lawrence W. Levine, for instance, cites these lines from an antebellum minstrel song:

> "My ole Missis promise me
> When she die she'd set me free;
> Now ole Missis dead an' gone,
> She lef' ole Sambo hillin' up corn." (192–93)

Now compare these lines heard during the Depression:

> "My ole mistress promised me
> Before she died she would set me free. . . .
> Now she's dead and gone to hell,
> I hope the devil will burn her well." (193)

While the latter speaker's anger contrasts sharply with the first speaker's self-deprecatory language, the dialogic relationship between the passages is clear.

In African American poetry, riffing often involves transposing vernacular expressions into written poetry by repeating them (sometimes with subtle and not so subtle changes) onto the printed page. One detects an early example of riffing in Paul Laurence Dunbar's "When Malindy Sings," wherein Dunbar riffs upon the sound of Afro-vernacular English. Later, James Weldon Johnson and Langston Hughes built upon Dunbar's achievement by riffing upon the sermon and blues forms, respectively. Similarly, Margaret Walker's "Kissie Lee" attempts to represent the speaking voice by riffing on both the ballad form and black vernacular.

Toughest gal I ever did see
Was a gal by the name of Kissie Lee
The toughest gal God ever made
And she drew a dirty, wicked blade.[73]

More recent examples of riffing include Arthur Pfister's "Stagolee and Billy" and Sherley Anne Williams's "Say Hello to John."

Pfister's poem, like many traditional versions, narrates a conflict over a dice game between Billy and Stagolee, the proverbial badman in black lore who terrorizes unsuspecting blacks and white authorities alike. In Pfister's revision, however, violence is not naturalized. Stagolee shoots Billy down to maintain his reputation: "It's sorry and sad / It's a sin and a shame / —the way some folk gotta git they fame."[74] So from the outset of the poem, Pfister critiques the unquestioned violence in many traditional versions wherein Stackolee's[75] assaults extend to the Devil himself: "The devil turned around to hit him a lick / Stackolee knocked the devil down with a big black stick" (50). And given the concluding lines, "September 1990 / (A Tough Season)" (172), "Stagolee and Billy" might even be read as an allegorical representation of black machismo in New Orleans.

Unlike Etheridge Knight's "Dark Prophesy: I Sing of Shine,"[76] Pfister situates his riff within the local dimensions of black vernacular culture, just as black musicians in New Orleans interpret the blues idiom in terms of a local aesthetic. Hence, Pfister's subtitle, "a Sixth Ward tale," and references to such local sites as Gentilly Boulevard and the Dew Drop Inn. Like Sterling Brown's riffing in *Southern Road,* which I will discuss in chapter 4, Pfister riffs at once on two distinct toasts ("Stackolee" and "the Signifying Monkey") to create a poem that also riffs on the black speaking voice. After Billy insists that Stagolee has rolled eight, not seven, Stagolee resorts to a form of signifying called the dozens ("I did it with yo' sister all last year / for a hot sausage san'wich and a bottle of beer" [170]), just as the Signifying Monkey retaliates against his nemesis, the Lion, by implying that the Elephant has been signifying on him:

He talked about cha family in a helluva way
He talked about cha family till my hair turned gray,
Called your mama a coon, called ya daddy one too,
Said I'll be goddamn if you don't look like one too.[77]

That the majority of the insults are directed toward women points up the problem of gender in Afro-vernacular culture.

Of course, it is not always possible to find a specific song/poem that serves as a creative model. There are a number of possible reasons for this: (1) many albums have gone out of print; (2) the poet may have revised a specific form rather than a particular song; or (3) the poet may have selected the human voice as a creative model. In Williams's "Say Hello to John," the reader who is familiar with black speech patterns is struck by the success with which the poet is able to represent the spoken voice. Having informed the reader of her earlier inability to recognize the symptoms of her imminent delivery, the pregnant young woman now says,

Second time it happen, even she
got to admit this mo'n pee.
And the pain when it come, wa'n't bad
least no mo'n I eva expect to see[.][78]

Note that "happen" is the vernacular equivalent of the Standard English word "happen*ed.*" The omission of the -ed reflects a tendency among black speakers to indicate tense within the context of a sentence.[79] As Geneva Smitherman points out, context signals time: "the same verb form serves for both present and past tense, as: *The bus pass me up last week,* but also: *The bus pass me up every day*" (26). In addition, the deletion of the /r/ sound in "mo'n pee" and the /s/ sound in "wa'n't bad" reflects the speech patterns of many black speakers. Thus, the poem's appeal is based upon the extent to which it approximates what readers identify as the sound of the speaking voice.

Epistrophy: The Performance of Cultural (Re)Memory

Because of the specific type of pastiche that characterizes this category, I have chosen epistrophy as a trope for this kind of formal revision. According to *Webster's Dictionary,* "Epistrophe" refers to the "repetition of the same word or expression at the end of a succession of phrases, clauses, or sentences for rhetorical effect." My decision to spell the word differently is prompted by Thelonius Monk's tune "Epistrophy,"[80] in which he provides listeners with what might be an instance of musical self-reflexivity wherein the pianist repeats certain sounds at the end of a phrase or riff. In "Epistrophy," the riff, which comprises a significant portion of the tune, is antiphonal. The response part of the riff is a slightly different version of the call or first phrase.

The word "epistrophy" suggests a unique African American style of cultural production that is both vernacular and sophisticated. For instance, the dances Monk performed counterclockwise around the piano recalls the ring shout, an antebellum religious ceremony that continues today in black churches. Yet his musical ideas, which were often expressed in rhythmic patterns that *seemed* out of tune, were as complex as those of any of his contemporaries.[81] Because Monk respected the aesthetic ideas developed in the margins of American culture, he was able to create a new approach to the piano that emphasized percussive effects; sometimes he even pounded his forearms on the piano. Wynton Marsalis explains: "'[Monk] invented an entire technique for the piano because the European approach was not sufficient for what he wanted to do. Monk was focused on the sound that has its basis in the blues, and everything he did took direction from that.'"[82] Marsalis's observation demonstrates black musicians' admiration of Monk's style, yet it is interesting to note that, like many blues poets, Monk has been criticized for having poor technique.[83]

As a trope, epistrophy involves a different kind of pastiche. Rather than imitating particular forms or expressive styles to create poems, epistrophy refers to a creative process that reflects and refracts African American cultural experiences by combining a wide range of forms, images, titles, lyrics, quotations, and names to create a poetic collage. An important component of epistrophy involves words that are particularly pertinent to African American history. But while Stephen Henderson calls such terms "mascon words," I prefer to call them "terms of cultural (re)memory." "Certain words and constructions," Henderson writes, "seem to carry an inordinate charge of emotional and psychological weight, so that whenever they are used they set all kinds of bells ringing, all kinds of synapses snapping, on all kinds of levels."[84]

Epistrophy subsumes riffing. Though the poets sometimes repeat forms or phrases, they are merely part of a larger poetic tapestry. Poets who employ epistrophy attempt to achieve artistic complexity by fusing their commitments to vernacular culture with their concerns for literary conventions. Like the poetry in the riffing section, epistrophic poetry is double-voiced: It renews the cultural (re)memory in both print and performance. However, epistrophy places more demands upon readers and listeners because of its compressed, allusive style. As Henry Louis Gates Jr. points out, in blues music one finds a similar artistic approach: "When playing the blues, a great musician often tries . . . to make musical phrases that are elastic in their formal properties. These elastic phrases stretch the form rather than articulate the form. . . . [A] dialogue [occurs] between what the listener expects and what the artist plays. Whereas younger, less mature musicians accentuate the beat, more accomplished musicians . . . feel free to *imply it*."[85] As in riffing poetry, epistrophies assume an informed audience, but here the cultural memory is summoned via suggestion. Forms and/or songs are often simulated, just as African American quilt makers have simulated antiphony with clashing colors. By using various techniques to establish rhythm, the poet, as Alvin Aubert observes, "plays the rhythm . . . contrapuntally against the remembered cadences of [the] folk source."[86]

Robert Hayden's "Runagate Runagate" provides an early example. The title of the poem is itself epistrophic. The poet creates tension by employing an oxymoron that combines two terms that are essential to African American cultural memory: "runaway" and "gatekeeper." The poem begins by describing the experience of escaping the plantation: "Runs falls rises stumbles on from darkness into darkness."[87] The absence of commas establishes a rhythm that suggests the anxiousness of an escape. Images of cultural memory, such as "hunters pursuing and the hounds pursuing" and "the night cold and the night long" (120), help to reinforce the runaway's anxiety and to maintain the rhythm established in the first line of the poem. The repetition of /h/ and /p/ sounds, as well as the repetition of "night," suggests the repetition that characterizes the black oral tradition.

Rather than riffing upon song forms, Hayden suggests various spirituals by fusing key words into the poem. The phrase "the river to cross" (120) evokes "One More River to Cross." "Many thousands rise and go" and "no more driver's lash for me" (121) recall "No More Auction Block," and "And before I'll be a slave / I'll be buried in my grave" (121) are lines from "Freedom Song."

Hayden also repeats, albeit ironically, notices of slave owners.

If you see my Pompey, 30 years of age,
new breeches, plain stockings, negro shoes;
if you see my Anna, likely young mulatto
branded E on the right cheek, R on the left,
catch them if you can, but it won't be easy. (121)

The brand images, as well as the words "my Pompey" and "my Anna," indicate both the slave's chattel status and the poet's opposition to such marginalization. The phrase "likely young mulatto" suggests both rape and the mythology of white supremacy. Her worth as a slave is based upon her potential to supply sexual pleasure, yet the term "mulatto" (from the Spanish word *mula*, which means "she-mule") directs readers' attention to the myth of white supremacy. Given that mules cannot bear offspring, the term illustrates an attempt to maintain the so-called purity of the white race by convincing Americans of purported dangers of interracial marriages.

African American vernacular English is also prominent in Hayden's poem—in the second section, for example, where the poet explores the runaway's psyche in language that blends Standard English with the vernacular.

> Moon so bright and no place to hide,
> the cry up and the patterollers riding,
> hound dogs belling in bladed air.
> And fear starts a-murbling, Never make it,
> we'll never make it. Hush that now,
> and she's turned upon us, levelled pistol
> glinting in the moonlight:
> Dead folks can't jaybird-talk, she says;
> you keep on going now or die, she says. (122)

The first line of the passage, with its zero copula, captures the rhythm of black vernacular, and the term "patterollers" is drawn from that lexicon. The line "no place to hide," in addition to alluding to the title of Sterling Brown's volume of poetry entitled *No Hiding Place,* suggests the trauma of the attempted escape and serves as a metaphor for the larger African American historical experience. However, the phrase "belling in bladed air" illustrates Hayden's attempt to explore the English language in its most diverse manifestations. In this light, the concluding line of the poem is especially significant: "Mean mean mean to be free" (122). The word "mean," which is repeated for musical and rhetorical effects, denotes both determination and vexatiousness, two indispensable qualities for a successful escape. In addition, Hayden's use of the zero copula evokes the sound of the black speaking voice, yet the repetition of /e/ sounds attests to his quest for a written art that simultaneously follows literary conventions while exploring the depths of Afro-vernacular culture.

In "My Name Is Arrow," Alvin Aubert revises a couplet that black roustabouts sang to ease the burden of their physical labor and to provide an outlet for themselves to express their candid feelings about their socioeconomic status: "'Oh Lawd, I didn't know / I had to bow so low'" (qtd. in Levine 250). Aubert's poem reads: "my old man bent down / so long so low / he turned into a bow."[88] Yet it is important to point out that the repetition here is not conscious. While the poem *appears* to be a parody of the song, Aubert actually had no knowledge of it.[89] Thus, "My Name Is Arrow" demonstrates the centrality of blues culture in Aubert's vision and the depth of Henderson's perception in relation to Afro-vernacular expressive practices. Naturally, one could argue that Aubert's unconscious riff is merely coincidental; however, I prefer to read it as a performance of cultural memory. If we consider the manner in which black dances have spread across the country *before* receiving airplay, we can imagine a sort of underground reservoir, as it were, in which privileged styles, words, and phrases are stored and later exchanged and/or revised within an African American cultural network.[90] The word "cat," for instance (recall Langston Hughes's "The Cat and the Saxophone"), is currently popular among black speakers and has come in and out of circulation several times since the 1920s. Similarly, young black speakers use the word "fly" as an adjective to denote beauty, but Larry Neal prefigured its current popularity in his poem "The Life: Hoodoo Hollerin' Bebop Ghosts."[91] Another example can be found in hip-hop. Many rappers have little knowledge of the blues idiom, yet they nonetheless revise the practice of improvisation by engaging in a form of extemporaneous rhyming called freestyling.[92]

In "My Name Is Arrow," Aubert repeats the work song's image of black male servility. But where the song brilliantly illuminates the limited parameters in which black subjectivity is constructed, Aubert's poem is more ambiguous. "My Name Is Arrow" not only describes the process of such constructions; it highlights black agency as well. The speaker's "old man" becomes a "bow" that responds to the repressive conditions that compel him to signify his submission to white hegemony by "bow[ing]" "so low." Many readers may understandably interpret the father as a prime example of political malformation, reenacting the dominant ideology to which he has been subjected by propelling his son in the direction of his own footprints. But while such an interpretation is not necessarily a misreading, it fails to address the significance of the central image in the poem: the bow is a potentially lethal weapon. Thus, it is ironic that the father, whether intentionally or not, becomes a resistive force through his son, Arrow. The ambiguity of the poem calls attention to its self-reflexivity. That is, with a sense of irony akin to the blues, the poem pokes fun at the very notion of arbitrarily ascribing fixed meaning and value to human beings, demonstrating that political opposition can come from the least likely source imaginable—one whose sociopolitical status is such that he has been forced to engage in obsequious displays of submission in order to survive. In claiming Arrow as his name, the speaker demonstrates his acute awareness of the dialectics of political opposition, that is, the transformational energy generated by the specific historicity of the father's bowing vis-à-vis Arrow's role as a fighter in the struggle to destroy the class/caste system that disfranchises black labor.

Another variation of epistrophy can be observed in Amiri Baraka's "Speech #38 (Or Y We Say It This Way)."[93] The poem opens with a list of key terms related to bebop.

OoBlahDee
Ooolyacoo
Bloomdido
OobopShabam
Perdido Klacto-
Veestedene
Salt Peanuts oroonie
McVouty
rebop[.] (258)

The passage, which is preceded by a dedication to Dizzy Gillespie and his song "Be Bop," reads like a foreign language to those who are unfamiliar with bop and illustrates the boppers' quest for autonomy. Gillespie recalls: "People who wished to communicate with us had to consider our manner of speech. . . . As we played with musical notes, bending them into new and different meanings that constantly changed, we played with words" (Gillespie with Fraser 281).

Similarly, Baraka attempts to use bop argot as a source of poetic diction. After the first line, which was a common scat phrase, he establishes a rhythm by repeating /u/ and /b/ sounds and alluding to key titles and of Gillespie recordings, such as "Ool-ya-koo," "Oop-Bop-Sha-Bam," "Bloomdido," "Perdido," and "Salt Peanuts." "[O]roonie/McVouty" alludes to both the saxophonist Jack McVey and Bulee (Slim) Gaillard, who coined the phrase. Including the epigraph, "bop" appears thrice, lastly in "rebop," which of course denotes bebop. In this way, Baraka approximates the angular rhythm of modern jazz.

The boppish rhythm, however, is not maintained throughout the poem. Beginning in the tenth stanza, the poem turns towards a conventional syntax, and it becomes clear that Baraka is narrating a poetic history of modern jazz while simultaneously creating myth based upon that history: "We dreamt Paradise / w/ you / Naima" (259). "Naima," a ballad named after Coltrane's first wife, is personified here as a sort of goddess of love who provides a soothing feeling similar to that experienced by the listener of the tune.

As Baraka constructs his myth, one finds more allusions to various people and places associated with jazz.

Brownie Red
Hollywood Hi Noon
Trane Lights
[. . .]

Yr heart
in Repetition
de Milos[.] (259)

Here one finds allusions to Coltrane, who played in Gillespie's band during the early 1950s, and the trumpeters Clifford Brown and Miles Davis. But "Brownie Red," also evokes Gillespie's recording of "Sweet Georgia Brown," during which he discovered that he could play "high B-flat" (241). Most specifically, though, "Brownie Red" recalls a tour of Southern California during which Gillespie remembers his famous fistfight with the singer Slim Gaillard for allegedly calling Gaillard an Uncle Tom (Gillespie with Fraser 242–44). The reference to Davis is particularly interesting, since it refers to Davis's "Venus de Milo," which appears on *Birth of the Cool,* a collection of recordings of his historic nonet.[94] Having established his reputation playing as a sideman with Charlie Parker, Davis collaborated with the arranger Gil Evans and initiated a new style of music dubbed "cool jazz" for which white musicians like Dave Brubeck would become famous, just as Benny Goodman was crowned the "King of Swing" after Fletcher Henderson had created big band music a generation earlier.

In the next sentence, Baraka directs our attention to two historical figures that are rarely yoked together—Thelonius Monk and Harry Truman:

Monk's Shades
made the tru/man
of a Hairy
Square
symbol
in faded corniness. (260)

Though Truman is often remembered as a populist president, the view from "Monk's shades" suggests otherwise. Like Langston Hughes roughly forty years earlier in "Ballad of the Landlord,"[95] Baraka poses the question: From what and/or whose point of view does the public view the relationship between workers and the elite? The ideas inscribed in Monk's dress and musical style reveal Truman as a committed defender of the very social system that denied Monk a cabaret card, which effectively rendered him unemployed.[96] As the house pianist at Minton's Playhouse, Monk had asserted great influence on the jam sessions that led to the formation of bebop, which functioned as aural calligraphy[97] that challenged the official historical narrative, albeit in the medium of sound: "Horns / of our / description" (260).

As the poem progresses, the reader encounters the poet reflecting upon the nightmare of the "Imperial Ghost" (260), that is, American imperialism and the "ignorance" (261) requisite to ensure that it remains unquestioned. The ghost image suggests obscurantism and the perpetuation of myths that are manifested in the construction of an American epistemology that excludes African Americans, Native Americans, Latinos, and women. Here the rhythm changes again, and Baraka, in a self-reflexive maneuver, refers to his own "Scatting" and preference for a poetics that emphasizes performance.

> Rhythm
> Rapping, capping
> hand
> slapping
> Black Poet
> Chanting
> to the 1st fire. (262)

Like his bebop heroes, then, Baraka has developed an alternative aesthetic to meet the needs of his audience. In addition to painting a visual script, his poetry "boogie[s]" (262). To underscore his point, he engages in epistrophy, repeating two words from the African American vernacular: "rapping" and "capping" (262). While most readers are familiar with the word "rapping," which, in the sense that Baraka uses it, denotes talking, "capping" may be more elusive. As a form of signifying, capping involves censure. "The point," according to Geneva Smitherman, "is to put somebody in check, that is, make them think about and, one hopes, change their behavior" (121). In this light, one can argue that "Speech" caps upon the American literary establishment. Which is to say, Baraka wants the members of the literary establishment to reconsider their concepts of poetry so that poetry that "boogie[s]" can be included. Hence, Baraka's reference to "Chanting" (262).

Cutting Sessions: The Incarnation of Secular Priesthood

The decision of many blues poets to use voice/instrument techniques constitutes the most radical challenge to literary conventions in the history of black poetry. However, since critics have been unable to imagine an alternative to a print-centered poetics, they have tended to ignore the artistic possibilities implied therein. Such indifference reflects a class bias that has a distinct history. As Raymond Williams points out, literature has always been associated with social privilege: "In its first extended sense . . . it was a definition of 'polite' or 'humane' learning, and thus specified a particular social distinction. . . . [that expresses] a certain (minority) level of educational achievement. This carried with it a potential and eventually realized an alternative definition of *literature* as 'printed books.' . . . [But] if literature was reading, could a mode written for spoken performance be said to be literature, and if not, where was Shakespeare?"[98] The implications for black poetry should be clear. Since literature, as a property reserved for the elite, signified the consumption and production of printed books, how could writers create literature for a disfranchised people who tend to communicate ideas most effectively via aural calligraphy?

Many blues poets have responded by following Neal's injunction to develop a poetics based upon African American music and/or sermons. Rather than a poetics characterized primarily by pastiche, like other modes of blues poetry, the poetry I will examine here constitutes an incarnation of the blues musicians and preachers. Even poets who have matured after the movement and expressed ambivalence toward many of its precepts have written blues poetry of this type that defies traditional criticism, which typically fails to take into consideration the function of sound in performance.[99] New methods of criticism are necessary to examine this poetry adequately.[100]

However, before I describe the critical approach I will adopt, I want to make some general remarks about the poetry and its relationship to the concept of a secular priesthood. Given the blues musician's role as a secular priest in black communities, blues poets' attempts to appropriate techniques from the blues tradition represent a quest for leadership executed in the style(s) of the black oral tradition. As D. H. Melhem argues, "Common to all are the strong incursions of Black music and the Black sermon, its poetry of the pulpit. Most of these poets have written prophetic works. At times they meld poetry and prose."[101] My concept of a secular priesthood trope is also based upon the enthusiastic responses from audiences and the great respect accorded to these blues poets. Yet just as blues musicians develop personal styles, so there are various shades of blues poets as well. The poets utilize voice/instrument techniques but differ in the manner in which they employ them. Some blues poems show almost no regard for the printed page, while others resemble the poetry described in the epistrophy section, with comparatively little emphasis on voice. Some poets, such as Amina Baraka and Quo Vadis Gex-Breaux, sing. Others, like Kalamu ya Salaam in his solo performances, approximate the sounds of instruments. Still others, like Jayne Cortez and Askia Toure, rely upon tonal inflection and rhythmic patterns, just as preachers and rappers[102] do in their performances.

Because of the aural nature of this poetry, I have found it useful to incorporate Smitherman's concept of tonal semantics into my model. Tonal semantics refers to an African American form of paralinguistics, which is a term that performance scholars use to describe means of communication that cannot be conveyed adequately in print. As Richard Bauman points out, "Paralinguistic features, by their very nature, tend not to be captured in the transcribed or published versions of texts."[103]

According to Smitherman, African Americans employ paralingusitic features to transmit various types of feelings and/or ideas through sound: "In using the semantics of tone, the voice is employed like a musical instrument with improvisation, riffs, and all kinds of playing between the notes. This rhythmic pattern becomes a kind of acoustical phonetic alphabet and gives black speech its songified or musical quality. Black rappers use word sound to tap their listeners' souls and inner beings in the same way that the musician uses the symbolic language of music to strike inward responsive chords in his listeners' hearts" (134). Smitherman's comments recall Finkelstein's observation that music can communicate ideas.[104] For this reason, I have selected the phrase "cutting sessions"[105] as a trope to examine how the poets use specific performative techniques to incarnate musicians and/or preachers.

The history of cutting sessions extends back to antebellum dance competitions at festivals where observers expressed their approval of dance couples by urging them to reach higher levels of performance. These contests and the particularly high standards set by the onlookers[106] anticipated the cutting sessions in which blues musicians later participated, as well as the battles and freestyle sessions in which rappers engage today.

In the lexicon of black musicians, cutting sessions or contests refer to duels between musicians in the heat of jam sessions. As Mezz Mezzrow says, "'The colored boys prove their musical talents in those competitions called cutting contests, and there it really is the best man wins, because the Negro audience is extra critical when it comes to music and won't accept anything second-rate. These cutting contests are just a musical version of *verbal duels.*'"[107] While "cutting" implies an adversarial relationship between musicians, the term denotes superior performance in the heat of a competitive battle that is itself a more intensified segment of a jam session. Miles Davis, for instance, recalls being "cut" by the trumpeter Kenny Dorham. Fearing that he had been upstaged, Davis sought confirmation in the audience from a fellow musician, Jackie McClean, who said: "'Miles, tonight Kenny is playing so beautiful you sound like an imitation of yourself.'"[108]

The comments by Mezzrow and McClean suggest the possibility of a critical practice from the perspective of a unique African American sensibility. Mezzrow's reference to "verbal duels" implies an isomorphic relationship between musicianship and verbal performance. Davis sought critical appraisal from McClean, who, as a fellow jazz musician, possessed the critical tools to interpret his performance. That is, McClean was an *informed* observer.

Similarly, critics of the blues poetry under consideration here should envision themselves as informed members of the writer's audience. While it is important to attend live poetry readings, I am really referring to a mode of analysis wherein critics attempt to examine the range and effectiveness with which poets employ oral/aural techniques. What are the specific qualities, critics might ask, that make the poetry appealing?

Haki Madhubuti was one of the most important poets of the Black Arts Movement, and his poem "But He Was Cool"[109] is a classic in the history of American literature. In the poem, Madhubuti transposes jazz into poetic form. "But He Was Cool" satirizes pseudorevolutionary black males who gave pretenses to nationalist philosophy while ignoring social change and focusing instead on accoutrements. The subtitle, "or: he even stopped for green lights," indicates a lack of progression that, in turn, implies a reactionary politics. The first two stanzas are prosaic, but the poet uses an ironic tone and black urban language for pyrotechnic effects. In the next stanza, however, Madhubuti uses jazz-related techniques to establish rhythm and augment his parody.

> woooooooooooo-jim he bes so cool & ill tel li gent
> > cool-cool is so cool he was un-cooled by other niggers'
> > > cool
> > cool-cool ultracool was bop-cool/ice box cool so cool cold
> > > cool
> > his wine didn't have to be cooled, him was air conditioned
> > > cool
> > cool-cool/real cool made me cool—now ain't that cool
> > cool-cool so cool him nick-named refrig-erator. (24)

The poet improvises riff-style upon the word "cool." That is, Madhubuti repeats it with various twists and turns, building upon each repetition until a peak of creative virtuosity and emotional intensity is achieved.

Despite its brief duration, Madhubuti's riff-style improvisation demonstrates the sheer power of the best poetry of the Black Arts Movement; it gives testimony to a viable poetics based upon the blues tradition. (It is important to bear in mind that Margaret Walker's "For My People" is a more extended version of the same style, though it does not require an equivalent degree of vocal dexterity to perform.)

Madhubuti reserves his most controversial idea for the conclusion of the poem. Though he excludes the southern component of the Civil Rights movement and thereby creates a regional hierarchy, Madhubuti nonetheless creates a novel framework in which to read blackness. In doing so, he illustrates why Black Arts writing is still taboo in academia today:

> after detroit, newark, chicago &c.,
> we had to hip
>   cool-cool/ super-cool/ real cool
>   that
> to be black
> is
> to be
> very-hot. (25)

Although Robert Farris Thompson has demonstrated that coolness was a key precept in traditional African societies, the material conditions in America shaped the form in which African Americans have revised the notion. At issue is the lack of a black/brown base with which to control a superstructure wherein ideas are created and disseminated. According to Thompson, coolness was "so heavily charged . . . with ideas of beauty and correctness that a fine carnelian bead or a passage of exciting drumming may be praised as 'cool' "[110] Madhubuti situates "But He Was Cool" within the historicity of coolness and (re)constructs it in terms of agency. And while some readers might argue that the passage is essentialist, I think the opposite is true: Madhubuti suggests that the black masses have waged a struggle of affirmation, not resignation.

Madhubuti's "But He Was Cool" marks a transitional moment in the development of an incarnation of secular priesthood. The recent work of Quo Vadis Gex-Breaux demonstrates a fuller realization of blues poetics. Though her poetry closely resembles that which is described in the epistrophy section, her style of tonal semantics requires a criticism that examines the function of voice, and it exemplifies a blues poetry that is truly liberating in its concerns for race, class, and gender.

In her poem "Jazz Rain,"[111] Gex-Breaux describes a jazz vocalist's experiences in narrative form. The title recalls a special feature of the blues tradition, the ability to evoke a local experience within the context of a personalized style. The combination of the words "jazz" and "rain" suggest the musical tradition as well as the natural environment of New Orleans. Gex-Breaux's ability to evoke a specific geography approximates one of the hallmarks of blues singing. The poem opens with oxymorons that reflect blues lyrics' ability to contain contradictions:

> She had a kind of classy coarseness
> like raw silk
> a kind of open earthiness
> without being dirt[.] (22)

The singer's "classy coarseness" suggests the raucous quality of blues music, whose premium on style lends itself to elegance. The reference to "earthiness" implies a funkiness that is also dignified. In linking "coarseness" with sophistication, Gex-Breaux, like Jayne Cortez, challenges hegemonic depictions of working-class black women and Afro-vernacular culture by exploding the mythology that equates workers with cultural deficiency.

Gex-Breaux's use of tonal semantics begins in the third stanza, where onomatopoeia evokes the New Orleanian landscape:

> She grew up with water sounds
> split   splat   splat
> on tin roofs
> soft tappings on bare window panes
> tip   tip   tip
> after heavy cloudbursts[.] (22)

The alliteration of /sp/ sounds and repetition of the "tip" image simulate the pitter-patter of raindrops. But in addition to recalling the climate of New Orleans, Gex-Breaux also uses the rain imagery to simulate the percussive quality of blues music. Note the music suggested by "water sounds" upon "tin roofs" and "window panes." The intricate patterns recall the sound of jazz and induces "laughter / that fell like jazz rain." In addition, the "tin roofs" image signifies the economic deprivation against which the singer and her community must struggle. Like most blues singers, Gex-Breaux does not offer solutions to the economic problems but describes the experience in a manner that seduces her audience to question traditional accounts of American democracy.

Given the historical misrepresentation of black culture, it is not surprising that the singer's music has been misunderstood. When "she sang her own harmonies,"

> Choice few could hear her music
> read the notes to which she danced
> hers was too cloistered an intellect
> to teach steps meant only for the select few[.] (22)

Gex-Breaux uses irony to subtly address the problem of gender. Though the singer's aesthetic is oriented toward mass appeal, few can read her aural calligraphy. Just as singers like Billie Holiday "danced alone and empty for hours," so Gex-Breaux's character must confront the contradiction of observing a male-centered audience that has been constructed in such a manner as to dance to the music of her voice without listening to its signification concerning experiences particular to women.

Gex-Breaux's decision to employ tonal semantics in her blues poetry stems from her belief in the poetry's potential to produce "human transformation" by touching her audience's spirit.[112] At times, however, words are not sufficient;[113] hence, her recourse to tonal semantics, as in the description of her own (blues) character:

> plish   plish   plish
> do wa-a-a-a-a-a[.] (22)

Though Gex-Breaux has expressed an antipathy for the use of expletives and slogans that characterized much of Black Arts poetry, her approximation of scatting represents a fruition of Neal's dream of a popular poetry that describes the black cultural experience in a style that illustrates its distinctiveness.

Kalamu ya Salaam illustrates another version of an incarnation of secular priesthood. Salaam's poetry reflects an oppositional politics and a radical challenge to literary conventions. Some critics would term his poetry pamphleteering, but insofar as the word implies that Salaam has no idea of craft it is quite incorrect. He has a distinct artistic method, but he reconceptualizes definitions of both poetry and artifact by collaborating with musicians on compact disc. Since Salaam considers the words of his poems as lyrics,[114] I have transcribed passages of the poem in a manner that suggests the rhythms and actual sounds of his voice. I have italicized the words or syllables of emphasis and spaced words and lines to provide a clearer idea of the actual sound of the poem.

The poet opens by stating his title, "Congo Square,"[115] a historic site so named by the Bakongo and other Africans who comprised the majority population in New Orleans.[116] There slaves were allowed to perform music and dances that were prohibited elsewhere in America. First, Salaam acknowleges the presence of Native Americans, who were displaced by African Americans: "The colonizers came and pushed aside our hosts / And introduced us in *chains*." The stress upon "chains" attracts listeners' attention and helps Salaam seduce them into confronting the history of slavery. Yet Salaam's belief that the slaves never fully accepted their objectification as chattel is reflected in the lines:

> we   some*how* and the *how* of our somehow persuasive methodologies is
>   not clear at this moment, the *how* is
> not clear, the *how* of our persuasive methodologies
> worked is not clear at this moment, but nevertheless,
> even as slaves, we crafted and created a space, where
> we   could be   free   to   be   we[.]

Salaam creates a riff chorus by repeating "how." The word also reflects his belief that genuinely oppositional cultural production cannot be based solely upon content. Style, too, is important in challenging the dominant social order. Note that the phrase "persuasive methodologies" is prosaic and illustrates Salaam's unabashed mission of propaganda. For most critics, this posture would disqualify the piece as a poem, and in print it bears little resemblance to conventional poetry.

However, Salaam employs tonal semantics and plays the inflection of his voice against the rhythms of the drummers. As the riff chorus intensifies, the conga players, whose collective voice as accompanists had functioned to accent the lyrics, begin to intensify their playing, building in emotional intensity until the soloist and the rhythm section become an ensemble by the end of the passage.

In his effort to reconstruct black fragmentation wrought by American colonization, Salaam suggests the viability of a style of life that emphasizes emotion and spirituality that have been repressed, ironically, by religious forces. More specifically, he employs a pun to emphasize the political implications of the cross symbol, which recalls: (1) the memory of the Middle Passage; (2) the imposition of Christianity; and (3) the development of capitalism. Salaam describes capitalism as an economic system that required the destruction of so-called primitive religions and languages. Thus, it constitutes a betrayal of humanity—the ultimate "cross" that intersects the preceding "crosses" that culminate in Herrenvolk democracy:

> which re*fuses* to   recognize
> the spirituality of *life*

which re*fuses*   to recognize
the spirituality   of *life*
and celebrates death
with *crosses* and *crosses*
double and *triple* crosses, the *mid*dle   passage
the *first* cross
Christianity,   the *double* cross
and *capitalism,* the ultimate triple *coup* de *grace* cross
of our captivity.

Again, Salaam uses the riff chorus to establish rhythm. As in the sermon, he employs hemistich phrases that may appear irregular in scripted form but sound regular when spoken.[117] Equally important, Salaam's use of tone inflection belies the apparent simplicity of the passage.

While much of conventional literature relies upon subtlety, which requires repeated readings for understanding and memory, Salaam strives for an affective poetics not unlike affective preaching, which allows the listener to experience the poem sensually and thereby gain a sense of understanding through memory. As Gerald Davis points out, "The power of the performance moves beyond the walls of the auditorium. . . . As in church, the spiritual essence . . . of the performance may well be carried into the days and weeks following the actual performance as those who experienced [it], or those who have reports of [it], discuss it, evaluate it, and relive it."[118] Similarly, the ideal poetic performance moves the audience to physical and/or audible response not unlike a blues musician. (Audience members at the 1996 Black Arts Festival in Atlanta, for instance, responded to Salaam's performance, which was filled with paralinguistic approximations of the saxophone, flute, and piano, with a standing ovation.)

Salaam's singular achievement in "Congo Square" stems from the fusion of two local vernacular traditions: Salaam, who was expected to replace his grandfather in the pulpit,[119] extends the oral tradition, while the conga players preserve a local drumming style. Thus, he achieves a new level of complexity, since interacting with musicians increases the difficulty of performing poetry. At perhaps the most controversial point in the poem, Salaam and the drummers reach a pinnacle of emotional intensity when Salaam ends a sentence with "drums":

our african *gods*
have not been o*bliterated*
they have merely re*treated* re*treated* in side the beat
of us, un*til*

```
we          are ready to release them into
a           world          we          re          cre          ate. a world herald by
       the beat
beee, beat being beating being, of black          heart
drumsss. heart          beat, heart               beat, heart          be at
this          place, at          this place,          be          heart be be          be
we          beating, place          in          new          world          space,
       beating[.]
```

When Salaam changes his inflection and establishes a different rhythm by punning, the drummers respond by decreasing their tempo, while Salaam creates a riff upon the word "be," varying the sound and rhythm in an antiphonal manner. It is also noteworthy that Salaam's riff represents self-reflexivity. Here he demonstrates his belief that the most effective means of mobilization—and hence, social change—is to incarnate the musician. In Salaam's conclusion, "beat, be, be, beat / rememba, rememba, rememba," even his language, that is, the deletion of "er," reflects an African American style of expression.

The political import of the foregoing passage raises another issue. A superficial reading might render a mythology of nationalism, that is, a romantic past that neglects the construction of Africa as a concept and an adherence to an outmoded religious system. However, Salaam's passage is a blues statement par excellence. Like Larry Neal, he interprets the emotion and spontaneity in black music as summonings of orishas.[120] Though he does not know his specific ancestral lineage because of the history of slavery, Salaam understands that his method of artistic expression would not exist without African religious practices, such as the possession phenomenon.[121] For Salaam, aural calligraphy exemplifies an African-derived sensibility that is manifested in "new world space."

4   Early Blues Poetics: Riffing
in Sterling Brown's *Southern Road*

BESSIE SMITH'S RECORDING OF "Gimme a Pigfoot" can serve as a metaphor for Sterling Brown's approach to blues culture in *Southern Road*. Where
previous renditions were mere showbiz pop tunes, Smith infused it with a
blues quality.[1] She complemented her concern for style—both in terms of
her sound and in her attire—with an equally impressive dedication to her
audience and a sense of courage that prompted her once to confront the
Klan. Like Smith, Brown revised popular forms, demonstrated a dedication
to his audience, and displayed courage in championing the cause of black
peasants in America.

It is fitting that Sterling Brown identified himself as a New Negro and
distanced himself from the concept of the Harlem Renaissance. The focus
on Harlem denied the richness of the rural black culture in the South where
Brown had discovered the sources for his art. More importantly, the New
Negro movement was one of resistance. Black soldiers had fought valiantly
for democracy abroad in World War I only to be denied first-class citizen-
ship upon returning home. The number of lynchings approached that of the
1890s, and the Ku Klux Klan had gained in popularity. But there were also
requitals. Riots occurred in Longview, Texas, Washington, D.C., and Chicago.
Hence, Rollin Harte quipped, "'The New Negro: you hit him, and he strikes
back.'"[2] Of course, African Americans had fought against unfair treatment

since European ships arrived on the coasts of Africa. What was different in the late 1910s and 1920s was a new sense of collective consciousness and maturity. W. E. B. Du Bois illustrates this new fighting spirit in an essay entitled "Returning Home": "'we are cowards and jackasses if now that the war is over we do not marshal every ounce of our brain and brawn to fight a sterner, longer, more unbending battle against the forces of hell in our own land. *We return. We return from fighting. We return fighting.*'"[3]

At the same time, however, this consciousness was framed largely in Eurocentric terms. The conservative essayist George Schuyler's comment that African Americans were no more than "'lampblacked Anglo-Saxon[s]'" (qtd. in Lewis 192) was a bit extreme, but the truth is that many African Americans despised Afro-vernacular culture, particularly blues music. The black elite's antipathy toward black music was nothing new (173). But this was a new age, a time for blacks to claim their rightful status as American citizens, and such a claim required sophistication—which meant the symphony, certainly not Bessie Smith or even Louis Armstrong. As Paul Oliver points out, "To the 'New Negro' and most of all to the Black recently arrived from the South who was earnestly seeking to acquire the worldly Northerner's veneer of sophistication, there were overtones of the 'Uncle Tom' element in the blues. Southern blues, folk music and talk, jive speech, and other creative forms that reinforce the morale of the under-privileged signified an acceptance of segregation and may even have appeared as devices that gave it support."[4] Even James Weldon Johnson, whose *God's Trombones* had demonstrated the poetic possibilities of black folk culture, declared in 1931 that dialect could only produce pathos and humor.[5]

Brown, however, was shrewd enough to reconceptualize sophistication in terms of the elegance of blues music, and he understood that the real "Uncle Toms" were those who embraced the forms of the dominant society simply because they were ashamed of the people who created the blues culture. Writing less than twenty years after *The Birth of a Nation* appeared, Brown, as Joanne Gabbin points out,[6] understood the politics of representation: the degree to which a marginalized group is misrepresented is directly related to its subjugation in real life. Thus Brown's question was, how could he help build a literature to describe cultural history from the viewpoint of a largely illiterate people?

His challenge was to create a new poetic language that captured the feelings and insights of his people. Hughes's *Weary Blues* (1926) and *Fine Clothes to the Jew* (1927) proved that vernacular expression and minstrelsy are not synonymous. However, while Hughes's poetry represented urban black culture,

Brown sought to depict black folk life in the rural South. More specifically, he sought to penetrate the psyche of black southern peasantry. For Brown, this entailed experimenting with a wider selection of forms than Hughes. "'Dialect, or the speech of the people,'" Brown said, "'is capable of expressing whatever the people are. And the folk Negro is a great deal more than a buffoon or a plaintive minstrel. Poets more intent upon learning the ways of the folk, their speech, and their character, that is to say better poets, could have smashed the mold. But first they would have had to believe in what they were doing.'"[7]

Brown's search for what Lorenzo Thomas calls an "authentic poetic voice"[8] of southern black peasants led to a blend of radical politics and mimetic revisions, that is, riffing on black oral and aural forms. In "Odyssey of Big Boy," Brown riffs on the black vernacular speaking voice and the ballad form to counter the misrepresentation of itinerant black workers. In his essay "Negro Characters as Seen by White Authors," Brown quotes Thomas Nelson Page, who says of black freedmen: "'for the most part, [they] are lazy, thriftless, intemperate, insolent, dishonest, and without the most rudimentary element of morality.'"[9]

As a title, "Odyssey of Big Boy" blends the name of the Greek hero with that of the bluesman Big Boy, who helped initiate Brown in his firsthand study of the black lore in and around Virginia Seminary.[10] In referring to Greek and African American art simultaneously, Brown provides an important clue to his own creative process. Just as bluesmen like Big Boy spoke English according to African grammatical rules, so Brown interprets the Western concept of literature in a uniquely African American style.

"Oddysey of Big Boy" should be read as a praise-poem for the heroic exploits of black workers: hence, the reference to Odysseus. Given their limited social mobility in the 1930s, the very idea of finding heroism among black workers is an act of resistance. At the outset of the poem, the persona evokes the folk heroes Casey Jones and Stagolee and expresses his desire to be with men like these when he dies. The persona then begins his odyssey:

> Done skinned as a boy in Kentucky hills,
>   Druv steel dere as a man
> Done stripped tobacco in Virginia fiel's
>   Alongst de River Dan
>   A longst de River Dan[.][11]

The "skinning" image reflects Big Boy's rural locale. "Skinning," in black vernacular, often refers to swimming nude in water holes—away from man-made beaches and swimming pools. But here the term probably refers to mule skinning.

Brown locates his representation of black speech within the specific historicity of rural Afro-linguistic practices. Mark Sanders has cautioned against misreading Brown as a sort of romantic folk poet.[12] But while I accept the thrust of his point, I contend that it is possible to read the Harvard man's self-conscious positioning within Afro-vernacular as an indication of his political identification with black peasants and his struggle against the bourgeois superstructure in America. Given the poetic form with which Brown is experimenting, his employment of "Done skinned," for instance, rather than the Standard English phrase "I have skinned," reveals the material conditions under which Big Boy toils and therefore exposes the contradictions that confine him to such an existence.

In its stanzaic construction, "Odyssey of Big Boy" does not follow the typical four-line stanza pattern. While Brown uses the abcb rhyme scheme that is typical of ballads, he riffs on the John Henry ballad, which consists of five-line stanzas that conclude with two repeating lines.

> When John Henry was a little fellow,
> You could hold him in the palm of your hand,
> He said to his pa, "When I grow up
> I'm gonna be a steel-driving man.
> Gonna be a steel-driving man."
>
> When John Henry was a little baby,
> setting on his mama's knee,
> He said, "The big bend tunnel on the C. & O. Road
> Is gonna be the death of me,
> Gonna be the death of me."[13]

In addition to enacting resistance by his reshaping of the ballad form, Brown adopts John Henry as a model for resisting misrepresentation. Part of John Henry's appeal is that he is a cultural rebel. Though he does not resist white authority, his conceptualization of his own identity compels him to engage in symbolic battle against the white world.

> John Henry said to his captain,
> "A man ain't nothing but a man,
> But before I'll let dat steam drill beat me down,
> I'll die wid my hammer in my hand,
> Die wid my hammer in my hand."[14]

His bulging biceps notwithstanding, John Henry is not unlike other folk heroes, such as Brer Rabbit and The Signifying Monkey, who triumph against insurmountable odds. What is unique about John Henry is that the folk, as toilers of the soil, could interpret his victory over the steam drill as a triumph over technology and thereby reaffirm their own integrity.

Equally importantly, Brown fuses the tone of the blues song with the ballad form, creating a blues-ballad. As Gabbin says, "the blues-ballad combines the narrative framework of the ballad and the ethos of the blues" (159). Both "John Henry" and "The Odyssey of Big Boy" celebrate the labor of black workers, and both begin by recounting boyhood experiences. Unlike "John Henry," though, Brown personalizes his poetic narrative. The result is a comic-heroic narrative whose central character is not a nebulous, mythic hero but rather Big Boy himself, who describes his own exploits in the context of heroic myth.

The next stanza accentuates the realism that distinguishes Brown's work from the dialect poetry of Dunbar. Although there is a strand of humor here, there is no image of the minstrel. Rather, Brown describes Big Boy's experiences without idealizing him:

> Done mined de coal in West Virginia,
>   Liked dat job jes fine,
> Till a load o' slate curved roun' my head,
>   Won't work in no mo mine,
>   Won't work in no mo mine. (20)

The reader or listener is caught unsuspecting by the third line, which vividly describes the physical danger of working in a mine. Not surprisingly, Big Boy expresses his refusal to work in mines and demonstrates some control over his life.

More importantly, Brown debunks the myth of laziness and thriftlessness. Note, for instance, that Big Boy initially *enjoys* working in mines. Brown's point is that the economics of slavery have prevented black workers from attaining economic stability. Consequently, workers like Big Boy wandered from job to job. Having worked as a dishwasher, Big Boy expresses his distaste for the job: "Done busted suds in li'l New York, / Which ain't no work o' mine— / Lawd, ain't no work o' mine" (20). Big Boy emphasizes his choice for outdoor physical labor. While he could simply be expressing his preference for a kind of work, one might note a bit of male chauvinism in his repulsion toward dishwashing. It is not difficult to find the implication here that dishwashing is a type of labor that befits women better than men.

Big Boy's inability to find steady work makes it difficult for him to establish stable relationships with women. Roaming the countryside and traversing the cities, he has played the role of both two-timer and two-timee.

> Had stovepipe blond in Macon,
>   Yaller gal in Marylan',
> In Richmond had choklit brown,
>   Called me huh monkey man-
>   Huh big fool monkey man.
>
> Had two fair browns in Arkansaw
>   And three in Tennessee,
> Had Creole gal in New Orleans,
>   Sho Gawd did two time me—
>   Lawd, two time, fo' time me—
>
> But best gal what I evah had
>   Done put it over dem,
> A gal in Southwest Washington
>   At four'n half and M—
> Four'n half and M. . . . (21)

The foregoing passage, including the sly, sexual innuendo involved with "Four'n half and M," points up the problem of gender in Afro-vernacular culture generally and Brown's work in particular. James Smethurst has argued that Brown envisioned the vernacular in masculinist terms.[15] However, without contesting Smethurst's point, it is important to remember that realism itself is a restrictive mode of representation. Brown's objective in *Southern Road,* however problematic, was to show "whatever the people are," which includes their own contradictions. Naturally, one might pose the question: To what extent does Brown share Big Boy's views? Admittedly, Brown's representation of gender in such poems as "Long Gone" (23) reflects a masculinist viewpoint. But "Ma Rainey," as we shall see, was sufficiently stirring to prompt Angela Davis to quote it as part of an introduction to her discussion of Rainey "because it so successfully conveys the southern flavor of her appeal."[16] More fundamentally, the multiple relationships in "Odyssey of Big Boy" are symptoms of underlying social problems that contribute to tensions in sexual relationships. Note that John Henry's status as an itinerant worker also limits his ability to maintain a stable relationship. And while some readers might point to the preslavery origins of male privilege in traditional African societies, it seems abundantly clear that, in addition to problems related to ideology, capitalism's treatment of black workers as slaves and, later, a reserve labor force has only exacerbated conflicts between black men and women.

At the same time, it is important to understand that Brown is riffing when he catalogues Big Boy's sexual partners. In Bessie Smith's "Mama's Got the Blues,"[17] which anticipates Tupac Shakur's "I Get Around,"[18] the persona boasts of having twenty-one men in different localities: She has one in Atlanta, two in Alabama, three in Chattanooga, four in Cincinnati, five in Mississippi, and six in Memphis, Tennessee. Of course, one might argue that Smith's celebration of multiple lovers, which can be read as a politicized rejoinder to male singers like Big Boy, ameliorates Brown's failure to question Big Boy's boasting, but a more astute reading might allude to the ideological contestation inscribed in Afro-vernacular culture. Historically, many black people have resisted the Eurocentric notion of the mind-body bipolarity, and under capitalist conditions, this worldview is sometimes manifested in the form of infidelity.

At the conclusion of his narrative, Big Boy returns to the subject of death and expresses his desire to be with folk heroes like John Henry when he dies, thereby striving for immortality.

> An' all dat Big Boy axes
>   When time comes fo' to go,
> Lemme be wid John Henry, steel drivin' man,
>   Lemme be wid old Jazzbo. (21)

Big Boy is the quintessential secular man, an embodiment of the blues spirit. Though he interprets immortality as real, there are no religious references here. Big Boy is a sinner in the view of the Christian congregation, yet he has derived happiness from and is proud of his "sins." Thus, Big Boy envisions an afterlife that includes neither Jesus nor angels but rather such heroes as Stagolee, Casey Jones, and John Henry.

While John Henry's heroic feats represent the resistance of black workers, Stagolee and the urban hipster Jazzbo represent resistance as the legendary badman who is fearless against white authorities. In "Johnny Thomas," Brown creates a counterpart to Stagolee by riffing on the ballad and African American vernacular English to undercut the myth of the brute Negro. "D. W. Griffith," Brown writes, "in *The Birth of a Nation* made for Thomas Dixon a dubious sort of immortality, and finally fixed the stereotype in the mass-mind. The stock Negro in Dixon's books . . . is a gorilla-like imbecile, who 'springs like a tiger' and has the 'black claws of a beast.'"[19] Writing in the typical four-line stanzas with an abcb rhyme scheme, Brown constructs a narrative wherein readers and listeners witness the incubation of the black male lumpenproletariat:

> Dey sent John Thomas
> To a one-room school;
> Teacher threw him out
> For a consarned fool. (42)

Brown foregrounds the issue of cultural authority by describing the rigidity and arbitrariness of the public educational system, which allows John Thomas little opportunity to acquire formal education. The word "Dey" is important because it suggests anonymity. The persona, who is presumably a member of Johnny's community, does not know who controls the school system. The decision makers are a conglomerate of entities lumped into one word: "Dey." The community's occlusion from the decision-making process reflects the extent to which it is disfranchised.

Similarly, the "one-room school" reflects the stark inequities in the social system. Black children of all ages must attend school in a single room if they wish to acquire any education whatsoever. Furthermore, the meager funds provided by the system can only afford an incompetent teacher who demonstrates his or her lack of concern by calling him a "consarned" (confounded or damned) fool. Thus, Brown suggests that not unlike black youth today, young southern black males in the 1930s were faced with the option of either conforming to the dictates of a haphazard educational system, which usually meant sharecropping, or a life of crime.

The leadership that Johnny's father provides is also suspect. He is a drunkard who mistakes a bloody beating for discipline:

> His pappy got drunk,—
> Beat de boy good,
> Lashed his back
> Till it spouted blood. (42)

Having been failed by his educational and familial institutions, Johnny becomes callous. Having internalized this negative treatment, Johnny, like Stackolee, learns to gamble and play pool because these activities are more appropriate for "a consarned fool." That is, the teachers of these lessons welcome boys such as Johnny as students.

When Johnny gets involved with a "fancy woman" whose tastes are expensive, his desire to satisfy her financial appetite requires Johnny to continue gambling, and he eventually depletes his funds. Consequently, the woman leaves him, and he is confused:

De jack run low
De gal run out
Johnny didn't know
What 'twas all about. (42)

Johnny's lover agrees to come back to him on the condition that he get more money, so Johnny begins to steal. Unfortunately, he is less skilled as a thief, and he is caught and placed on the chain gang:

Johnny was a tadpole,
Sheriff was a eel,
Caught him jes' as soon
As he started to steal.

Put him on de chain gang,
Handled him cruel,
Jes' de sort of treatment
For a consarned fool. (42)

At this point in the poem, the line "For a consarned fool" has become a refrain that accentuates the absurdities of Johnny's life by sarcastically echoing the sentiments of white authorities.

The mule metaphor, which prefigures Zora Neale Hurston's in *Their Eyes Were Watching God*,[20] is appropriate in that it reflects the southern aristocracy's attempt to dehumanize Johnny. Like the slaves before him, Johnny's value can only be assessed in terms of his ability to work and produce profits. His fight with the prison guard and his refusal to conform to this expectation constitutes rebellion. He is therefore "cussed" as a recalcitrant mule. But since he is neither slave nor mule, Johnny must be put to death:

Dropped him in de hole
Threw de slack lime on,
Oughta had mo' sense
Dan to evah git born. (43)

One might have thought that the poem had exhausted all possibilities before this last stanza; after all, Johnny had already been haltered and hung. Yet the first two lines of this stanza emphasize the extent to which Johnny has been dehumanized. His body is merely "in de hole" without the dignity of a funeral. The "slack lime" suggests mortar and all of its deathly implications. The last two lines are even more powerful in that they suggest that Johnny was simply a victim of circumstances. The sarcastic tone highlights the ludicrousness of Johnny's life. Needless to say, individuals cannot choose parents, so it is utterly ridiculous to expect someone to have had "mo' sense" than to ever be born. Yet Brown suggests that this is the only way Johnny could have avoided injustice in America.

Brown's description of the chain-gang experience bears a striking similarity to the bluesman Memphis Slim's account of his experience in levee camps: "'Work you from can see to can't see. . . . You couldn't say you was tired and wanted a break 'cause they'd crack you upside your head with a club. Them straw bosses would beat you dead. Mister Charlie say, "Kill a nigger, hire another. But kill a mule you got to buy another."'"[21] Shackles and chains are, of course, by-products of slavery. The history of the twenty-pound ball and chain, for instance, extends as far back as the 1780s in Pennsylvania. Such was the horror of the chain gangs that men sometimes severed the tendons of their legs to avoid working on them.[22] Since slave masters found that blacks were more productive laborers when they sang, they did not object to it. And though blues music became the most popular art form in African American culture, the work song continued into the twentieth century. "Some of the worksongs," Amiri Baraka writes, "use as their measure the grunt of a man [or woman] pushing a heavy weight or the blow of a hammer against a stone to provide the metrical precision and rhythmical impetus behind the singer."[23] "John Henry Hammer Song" is such a song:

> Dis ole hammer—hunh
> Killt John Henry—hunh
> Twon't kill me, baby—hunh
> Twon't kill me.[24]

When one recalls that work songs prefigured the blues and that some work song lines resemble blues stanzas,[25] it is not surprising that Brown, in "Southern Road," riffs on both forms by fusing them to create a blues work song:

> Swing dat hammer—hunh—
> Steady, bo';
> Swing dat hammer—hunh—
> Steady, bo';
> Ain't no rush, bebby,
> Long ways to go. (52)

The persona has committed murder and received a life sentence:

> Burner tore his—hunh—
> Black heart away;
> Burner tore his—hunh—
> Black heart away;
> Got me life, bebby,
> An' a day. (52)

The word "Burner" refers specifically to gunfire, and the last line, "An' a day," suggests the hopelessness of ever joining the outside world. But it is also important to understand that the word "burn" refers to deception generally. In his selection of the term, Brown skillfully calls attention to the aggression and hot tempers that flared at jook-joints where blues musicians provided a release from the pent-up frustrations from long, hard work for low wages. At times, emotions spilled over into violence between jealous lovers or angry gamblers. In *Mules and Men,* Zora Neale Hurston observes a crap game that provides a context for understanding how such violence could occur:

> Office had the dice when I walked up. He was shivering the dice and sliding them out expertly.
> "Hah! good dice is findin' de money! Six is mah point."
> "Whut's yo' come bet?" Blue asked.
> "Two bits."
> "Two bits you don't six."
> Office picked up the dice stealthily, shook them, or rather failed to shake them craftily and slid them out. Blue stopped them. Office threw three times and three times Blue stopped them. Office took out his switchblade and glared at Blue.
> "Nigger, don't you stop mah dice befo' dey point."
> "You chokin de dice. Shake and lemme hear de music."[26]

Thus, blues people like the persona lived with the specter of violence hovering over them like dark rain clouds.

As the persona's song progresses, he describes the dissolution of his family that has presumably occurred as a result of his imprisonment. His daughter now works on "Fifth Street" as a prostitute; his son "done" left home; and his wife is "in de ward" awaiting the birth of a baby who will never know his or her father. When he shifts the focus to his own condition, he displays stoicism. Unlike John Thomas, the persona is the author of his own narrative: "The immediate impulse is toward survival, not resignation. By crafting a form that reshapes and recasts oppressive conditions, the speaker assumes a fundamental control over them and ultimately over his own life."[27]

As I mentioned in chapter 3, the vast majority of blues songs were not overtly political, but work songs often were. Jean Wagner says that "the entire spirit of revolt is snuffed out and transcended, since it is seen as useless."[28] But while Wagner is right to suggest the impossibility of physical revolt, he is mistaken in his assertion that his rebellious "spirit" has been killed. In practical terms, the persona is fully conscious of the implications that he is "double-shackled" with a "Guard behin'," and he understands that he is member of a colonized group:

> White man tells me—hunh—
> Damn yo' soul;
> White man tells me—hunh—
> Damn yo' soul;
> Got no need, bebby,
> To be tole. (52–53)

The persona, like John Thomas, is "cussed" but is allowed to live because he is willing to work like a mule. Unlike John, though, the persona can claim authority for his own experiences. As a singer, he uses song to confront the truth of his life: he is a sinner who cannot expect solace by going to heaven. Rather, he is a "Po' los' boy . . . Evahmo'." Thus, the music is not simply a stimulant for work but a blues song in work song form that allows the persona to maintain his sense of identity.

Brown's formal achievement in "Southern Road" deserves further comment. While it is true that he revises the work song form in general, it is also true that he riffs on work songs in "Southern Road":

> Told my captain—hunh
> Hands are cold—hunh
> Damn yo' hands—
> Let de wheelin' roll.[29]

Brown displaces the metonym "captain" with its referent, "white man," and performs a chiastic maneuver, reversing subject and object. Brown also substitutes "soul" for "hands" to emphasize the cruelty of white authorities. Similarly, the phrase "Po' los' boy" is a riff on "Poor Boy Long Ways from Home."[30]

Though Brown has been criticized for simplicity, his experiments with song forms have been complicated enough to confuse some readers.[31] Sterling Stuckey, for instance, has called "Ma Rainey" "perhaps *the* Blues poem."[32]

But while the poem is certainly informed by a blues aesthetic, Stuckey's statement must be qualified. "Ma Rainey" is not a blues poem in form. Unlike
poems such as "Tin Roof Blues" or "New St. Louis Blues," "Ma Rainey" is not
written in the standard aab blues form—or even a variation of it. Rather, "Ma
Rainey" is a blues-ballad.[33] But while Big Boy embodies the black cultural
spirit, here there is no central character or point of view. Instead, Brown, in
his attempt to depict the collective experience of blues people, varies the point
of view, narrowing the focus as the poem progresses. Brown opens "Ma
Rainey" by riffing on travel songs that bluesmen like Henry Thomas sang:

> I'm on my way but I don't know where,
> Change cars on the T.P.,
> Leaving Fort Worth, Texas,
> Going through Dallas,
> Hello, Terrell,
> Grand Saline,
> Silver Lake,
> Mineola,
> Tyler,
> Longview,
> Marshall,
> Little Sandy,
> Texarkana,
> And double back to Fort Worth[.][34]

Compare the opening of "Ma Rainey," listing the various regions of her audience:

> When Ma Rainey
> Comes to town,
> Folks from anyplace
> Miles aroun',
> From Cape Girardeau,
> Poplar Bluff,
> Flocks in to hear
> Ma do her stuff;
> Comes flivverin' in,
> Or ridin' mules,
> Or packed in trains
> Picknickin' fools. . . . (62)

The success of the section rests, in part, upon Brown's ear for Afro-vernacular cadence. "Fliver" is slang for an inexpensive car. In employing a deriv-

ative, onomatopoeic verb that suggests the rickety nature of the vehicle itself, Brown again recalls Hurston's keen observation regarding black speakers' penchant for transforming nouns into verbs,[35] which attests their desire
for action words.

In the next section, Brown narrows the focus on the folk themselves.
When filing into the hall, they converse among themselves, "jes' a-laughin'
an' a-cacklin', / Cheerin' lak roarin' water, lak wind in river swamps" (62).
The similes are characteristic of African American vernacular English and
help to create the lyricism that is the very stuff of the blues. Consider this blues
couplet: "'If you use my key, well you bound to love me some / Throw your
arms around me like a circle around the sun.'"[36] Or this metaphor from Hurston's *Their Eyes Were Watching God:* "If God don't think no mo' 'bout 'em
then Ah do, they's a lost ball in de high grass."[37] Whereas the first section lists
the cities from which the people come, the second reveals that despite living
in cities, the folk are forced to live in "river settlements" because the only work
available is located in "blackbottom cornrows" and "lumber camps."

Brown's rhythmic devices are also important. In addition to showcasing
a propensity for vivid imagery, the similes help establish a lyrical rhythm and
are characteristic of black folk expression. The repetition of "An some" functions in a manner similar to a riff chorus, setting the rhythm for the last
stanza of the section:

An' some jokers keeps deir laughs a-goin' in de crowded aisles
An' some folks sits dere waitin' wid deir aches and miseries,
Till Ma comes out before dem, a-smilin' gold toofed smiles
An' Long Boy ripples minors on de black an' yellow keys. (62)

When the focus shifts again, we find that the persona is a member of
Rainey's audience: he or she reflects its worldview. Here the poem describes
the role of the blues singer in the community:

O Ma Rainey,
Sing yo' song;
Now you's back
Whah you belong,
Git way inside us,
Keep us strong. . . . (63)

The persona's response is similar to that of a congregation member in
church. He or she acts as a witness who has been touched by the spirit and
thereby testifies to the emotional truth of the song. Such responses are common in audiences of both sacred and secular music. When audiences con-

sider a song to be particularly poignant, the people, as Jeff Titon points out, respond with "shouts of 'That's right' or 'Amen' or 'Tell 'em about it.'"[38] Rainey's ability to serve as a priestess for her community allows her to penetrate the people's exteriors and touch them spiritually, thereby providing catharsis that keeps them strong.

In the final section, the poet gives his own testimony to what Wynton Marsalis calls the "majesty of the blues." In a gesture that exemplifies the best of blues music itself, Brown fuses anecdote, a section from "Backwater Blues," and his own blues creation to illustrate how Rainey's music affects her audience.

> I talked to a fellow, an' the fellow say,
> "She jes' catch hold of us, somekindaway.
> She sang Backwater Blues one day:
>> It rained fo' days an' de skies was dark as night,
>> Trouble taken place in de lowlands at night.
>>
>> Thundered an' lightened an' the storm begin to roll
>> Thousan's of people ain't got no place to go.
>>
>> Den I went an stood upon some high ol' lonesome hill,
>> An' looked down on the place where I used to live.
>
> An' den de folks, dey natchally bowed dey heads an' cried,
> Bowed dey heavy heads, shet dey moufs up tight an' cried,
> An' Ma lef' de stage, an' followed some de folks outside." (63)

There were many songs written about the flood of 1927. Seven hundred thousand people were left homeless.[39] In some places, the water level rose to sixty-five feet, engulfing whole townships. Houses, cattle, and mules floated in the water.[40] Brown uses the historical tragedy as source material to illustrate the emotional bond between Rainey—and by extension, blues singers in general—and her audience. "The blues singer," Paul Oliver writes, "turn[s] his eyes on the inner soul within and record[s] his impressions and reactions to the world without."[41] Rainey's decision to interact with the people after the performance demonstrates her communion with them and helps us to understand her ability to attract audiences from Cape Girardeau, Missouri, to Mobile, Alabama.

What is most noteworthy about this section, however, is the complexity of Brown's riff on the blues form. Just as blues singers infuse passages of other songs into their own songs, Brown frames Rainey's blues with his own blues composition. The first three lines suggest both the early blues and the talking blues. Though there is no single repeated line, Brown employs the aaa rhyme scheme that marks the early blues. But the rhyme scheme is only a device for Brown's riff on the talking blues, which is, as Harry Oster says, "'semi-rhythmic speaking or a mixture of speaking and singing, accompanied by rhythmic guitar.'"[42] Of course, in Brown's version, there is neither singing nor guitar. But the repetition and compression in the first and second lines, respectively, point unmistakably to a blues aesthetic.

Though Gabbin claims that Brown "incorporates Bessie Smith's popular 'Backwater Blues'" (159), he does not so much incorporate Smith's song as riff on it. At least one quotation of Smith's song differs from the version in "Ma Rainey": "It thunders an' lightnin's an' the wind began to blow, / When it thunders an lightnin's an' the wind begin t'blow, / There's thousands of people ain't got no place to go."[43] Brown eliminates the first word of both lines. The stanza in Smith's text is composed in the standard twelve-bar structure, but Brown's version is comprised of couplets. Brown's version also differs in tense. While Smith's song is in present tense, Brown writes in past tense, which is better suited for the narrative qualities of the blues-ballad.

After his riff on "Backwater Blues," Brown returns to his talking blues riff. Here, however, in the most moving stanzas in the corpus of his poetry, Brown composes his own twelve-bar blues in the standard aab structure. The first stanza is a portrait of African American vernacular English. Notice the repetition of the subject and the /d/ sound instead of /th/. Like many of the best blues singers, Brown improvises in his repetition of the first line. The variation creates the illusion of an actual blues performance in which instrumentation is often employed in place of vocalization.

One of Brown's most important poems is "Strong Men," which signifies upon Carl Sandburg's "Upstream" by selecting the line "The strong men keep coming on" as his epigraph and then employing it as one of the riff choruses that set the rhythm in the poem. As Charles H. Rowell has pointed out, Brown adopts the cadence of the slave secular that catalogues the injustices of the slave experience:

> We raise de wheat,
> Dey gib us de corn;
> We bake de bread,
> Dey gib us de crust;
> We peel de meat,
> Dey gib us de skin;
> And dat's the way
> Dey take us in;

We skim de pot,
Dey gib us de liquor,
And say dat's good enough for nigger.[44]

Now compare the first section of "Strong Men":

They dragged you from homeland,
They chained you in coffles,
They huddled you spoon-fashion in filthy hatches,
They sold you to give a few gentlemen ease.

They broke you in like oxen,
They scourged you,
They branded you,
They made your women breeders,
They swelled your numbers with bastards. . . .
They taught you the religion they disgraced.

You sang:
    Keep a-inchin' along
    Lak a po' inch worm. . . .

You sang:
    Bye and bye
    I'm gonna lay down dis heaby load. . . .

You sang:
    Walk togedder, chillen
    Dontcha git weary. . . .
        The strong men keep a-comin' on
        The strong men git stronger. (56)

Rather than writing exclusively in blues stanzas, Brown employs blues devices to riff on the slave secular. The cataloging, written in Standard English, functions as a call not unlike the repeated lines in blues lyrics. The spirituals passages serve as responses. While the lines beginning with "we" and "they" are alternated in the slave secular, Brown varies the rhythm, making it more complex by playing the catalog of racial injustices contrapuntally against passages of spirituals.

It is appropriate that Brown selects excerpts from black music to describe the collective responses to victimization. In spite of the degradation, the people create songs that not only attest to their linguistic wit but also testify to a mental toughness that allows the folk to endure. They have been "dragged," "chained," "huddled," "broke[n] . . . in," "scourged," and "branded," yet they do not despair. Buoyed by their belief in sweet Jesus, the people cling to hope of a brighter future when they will not be forced to bear such "heaby load[s]."

When the focus shifts to (then) present-day conditions, there is a stark contrast in the division of labor between whites and blacks. "They" act as supervisors, ostensibly skilled in the art of direction. The folk, however, act as little more than serfs who must "[d]rive so much before sundown." Nonetheless, they maintain their dignity by taking pride in the work that they do:

> *You sang:*
>> *Ain't no hammah*
>> *In dis' lan',*
>> *Strikes lak mine, bebby,*
>> *Strikes lak mine.* (56–57)

The speaker returns to the past in the next stanza to cite still more atrocities suffered by the people. But there is a subtle, yet telling, variation here: *"They tried to guarantee happiness to themselves / By shunting dirt and misery to you"* (57). Whereas the speaker has previously spoken of contemporary occurrences or historical events, here he uses the term "tried." Brown suggests that class struggle is a dynamic phenomenon. Despite the concerted efforts of the southern oligarchy to repress the people into psychological submission and thereby maintain economic and political power by "buying off" relatively affluent blacks, the people persist, engaging in haunting guffaws that attest to their will to survive: *"They heard the laugh and wondered; / Uncomfortable, / Unadmitting a deeper terror"* (57). The "deeper terror," of course, is that the measures taken by southern whites are not sufficient to crush the spirits of the people—a fear that such persistence will lead to equality in spite of the myriad "Reserved for Whites Only" signs.

It is particularly interesting that, the poem's protest of racism notwithstanding, Brown never mentions blacks categorically. Notice, for instance, that the "strong men" refrain avoids direct reference to race. Granted, one can argue that, given the formal strategies of the poem, such a point is moot—that the speaker is clearly referring to blacks. However, it also seems clear that Brown is concerned with describing African American colonization within the context of internationalism.

The complexity of Brown's experiments is perhaps most clear in "Memphis Blues," wherein he analyzes the black community's response to crisis by applying a blues aesthetic to his fusion of secular rhyme, blues lyricism, and the sermon. The result is a sort of secular sermon rendered in a blues modality: a blues-sermon. Using the aba form (that is, text, elaboration of the text, and repetition of the original text) commonly found in sermons,[45] Brown creates a poem whose rhythmic qualities recall the sermon while adhering to a blues method. The poem opens in secular rhyme, recalling a number of cities that no longer exist:

> Nineveh, Tyre,
> Babylon,
> Not much lef'
> Of either one. (60)

Commonly associated with wickedness, the once great cities are now "ashes and rust." The obvious implication is that contemporary Memphis, which is associated with the luxury afforded by the southern elite, will eventually undergo a similar fate, since the earlier Memphis was destroyed "[i]n many ways." Thus, the speaker harbors no illusions concerning the indestructability of "[d]is here Memphis":

> Floods may drown it;
> Tornado blow;
> Mississippi wash it
> Down to sea—
> Like the other Memphis in
> History. (60)

In the second section, Brown employs call and response to riff simultaneously on the blues and the sermon. It is important to recall that despite the black church community's antipathy toward blues music (Mahalia Jackson's refusal to sing blues lyrics, for instance), blues musicians not only described their performances in religious terms, they also infused spirituals into their songs. Moreover, given Brown's concern for the community at large, it is appropriate that he draws from various forms, since they correspond to different segments of the community. Brown's preacher is asked: "Watcha gonna do when Memphis on fire, / Memphis on fire, Mistah Preachin' man?" And he responds: "Gonna pray to Jesus and nebber tire, / Gonna pray to Jesus, loud as I can, / Gonna pray to my Jesus, oh, my Lawd!" (60). The speaker's call, as Stephen Henderson has noted, is a riff on a formulaic Afro-vernacular phrase.[46] In the spiritual "What You Gonna Do?" various members of the community—sinner, brother, sister, mother, father—are asked repeatedly, "what you gonna do / when the world's on fi-er?" In "Honey O Babe,"[47] Big Bill Broonzy employs the same formula, shifting the locus to a pond that has gone dry. And the novelist John O. Killens recalls a couplet from his childhood: "'Whatcha gonna do when the world's on fire? / Run like hell and *holler,* "Fire!"' "[48] While the calls in the songs were usually riff choruses, Brown inverts the pattern by using the riff chorus as the response in which he worries the line three times. But Brown skillfully creats a miniature riff chorus of his own in the call. The first line is partially repeated in the second line, which specifically addresses the preacher. After this process is repeated in the next five stanzas of the section, the poem achieves a musicality whose rhythm is based upon the improvisation of the first and third lines of each stanza.

As is the case in "Ma Rainey," Brown suggests that in addition to rampant racism, the folk must also contend with the forces of nature that are also beyond their control. And like Ralph Ellison's Trueblood,[49] they will accept their painful fate, face it, and continue to live in the manner that they had previously. The preacher will preach; the lover will love; the musician will play music; the worker will build buildings; the drinker will drink; and the gambler will gamble.

But since the people receive few of the profits that are accumulated by the city, they are indifferent toward Memphis. They are natives to American soil, but like the blues themselves, they are scorned by the dominant society and treated as foreigners. Brown explores this dynamic further in the last section of the poem, riffing simultaneously on the secular rhyme and the standard blues song:

> Memphis go
> By Flood or Flame;
> Nigger won't worry
> All de same—
> Memphis go
> Memphis come back,
> Ain' no skin
> Off de nigger's back. (61)

Though the lines are actually rhymed couplets, Brown shortens them to maximize their bluesy quality.

The ambiguity of the last two lines allows for several interpretations. On the one hand, one might argue that the spirituals symbolize the eventual triumph of the forces of virtue over evil, symbolized by the now destroyed cities. On the other hand, one might argue with equal force that the speaker seems to be disillusioned with a Christianity that brings no life, no greenery, but only dust. Wagner offers another possibility when he says, "No doubt at times [the people] imagine God to be an ally, but this is mere illusion."[50]

While I do not disagree with Wagner's statement, I think he fails to consider the function of the spirituals in Brown's vision. Just as the spirituals in "Strong Men" illustrate the people's indomitable will to endure, so here Brown suggests that even after the day of reckoning, the folk will continue to fashion a life out of their living hell.

Another formal innovation that deserves critical attention concerns Brown's revision of the tall tale or, perhaps better, the "lie." Like the sermon form, many performers may feel the call, but relatively few can develop the nuances and subtleties necessary to command the attention and respect of black audiences. In the late 1920s, Brown met a waiter in Jefferson City, Missouri, who provided a basis for one of his most significant achievements: the introduction of the lie into modern literature with his series of Slim Greer poems. Of the persona in these poems and their real-life original, Brown remarks, "'He says I owe him some money because I shouldn't have taken his name'" (qtd. in Gabbin 136). In a maneuver that is typical of his creative process, Brown riffs on the lie and the ballad simultaneously, employing the latter as a mold to give shape to his hilarious narrative.

> Talkinges' guy
> An' biggest liar,
> With always a new lie
> On the fire

Tells a tale
Of Arkansaw
That keeps the kitchen
In a roar[.] (77)

Thus Brown describes one of the most effective psychic weapons that blacks have developed in America: the ability to laugh at the absurdities of Jim Crow society. Slim is especially funny because he can "lie" with a straight face about "passing" for white in Arkansas even though he is "no lighter / Than a dark midnight."

After he meets a white woman who thinks he is "from Spain / Or else from France," Slim is discovered by a "Hill Billy," who, upon hearing Slim playing blues on the piano, immediately suspects that Slim is an imposter:

The cracker listened
An' then he spat
An' said, "No white man
Could play like that. . . ." (78)

The irony is humorous yet cutting. The suggestion, of course, is that blues music is an African American expression. However, to make certain that Slim is black, that is, a "Nigger" and therefore devoid of any claim to civilization, the "Hill Billy" must cling to a sort of constructed ignorance. By suggesting that whites and blues music are mutually exclusive, the "cracker"[51] traps himself into a logic in which artistic incapability constitutes a badge of racial superiority.

The humor reaches a climax when the white woman, having been tipped off, now also suspects Slim:

> Crept into the parlor
> Soft as you please,
> Where Slim was agitatin'
> The ivories.
>
> Heard Slim's music—
> An' then, hot damn!
> Shouted sharp—"Nigger!"
> An' Slim said, "Ma'am?" (78)

The woman gives Slim a cultural test by calling him "Nigger" to find out whether he responds in a conditioned way. When he responds instantly, he reveals his identity, thereby failing the test. Consequently, he must now use speed, one of the traditional attributes of black tricksters, since he can no longer use wit as protection.

The wisecracks inscribed in black lies point up the dialectical nature of vernacular forms, and like the blues virtuoso Bennie Moten, Brown riffs on the lie in "Slim in Atlanta" to expose the ludicrousness of the Jim Crow legal system that "keep[s] all de niggers / From laughin' outdoors" (81). The laws reach a pinnacle of absurdity when one discovers the stipulation the southern aristocracy has established for blacks who wish to laugh outside their homes:

> Hope to Gawd I may die
> If I ain't speakin' truth
> Make de niggers do deir laughin
> In a telefoam booth. (81)

The disclaimer in the first line is a formula that liars use to increase the effectiveness of their performance. The ability of the liar to provoke a response with a line such as "I ain't lyin"[52] increases in proportion to the outrageousness of the lie.

Though he is no revolutionary, Slim is certainly a rebel. His very perception of the social conditions in Atlanta poses a threat to the "rebs," who warn him that the penalty for disobeying the laughter laws is death. But when he is pointed to a booth and sees the spectacle of "a hundred shines / . . . / In double lines," Slim is unable to contain his laughter:

Slim thought his sides
  Would bust in two,
Yelled, "Lookout, everybody,
  I'm comin' through!"

    Pulled de other man out,
      An' bust in de box,
    An' laughed four hours
      By de Georgia clocks. (81)

Slim is eventually escorted out of town when the state pays the railroad for the expenses: "Den, things was as usural / In Atlanta, Gee A" (82).

In capturing the language and psyche of characters such as Slim Greer and Big Boy, Brown elaborates upon the Afro-modernism of Langston Hughes and Jean Toomer. And yet to speak of an *Afro*-modernism is to trouble the waters surrounding normative conceptualizations of modernism. As we shall see in our discussion of Hughes in chapter 5, to discuss "modernism with any real sense of historical accuracy, one must speak, in effect, of 'modern*isms*,' several divergent, often competing strands of artistic and ideological expression for the same cultural moment."[53] "High modernists" like Ezra Pound and T. S. Eliot masked fascist politics within visual experiments that naturalized the confinement of the international working class. Modernists more concerned with foregrounding a radical politics—Van Wyck Brooks and Max Eastman among them—often deemphasized form, "pointing the conservative finger back at" the high modernist camp.[54] But Brown envisioned formal innovation as an artistic strategy to challenge hegemonic representations of the black masses. And though poets like Hughes, Margaret Walker, and Brown's protégé, Sherley Anne Williams, would later revise Brown's version of modernism, *Southern Road* constituted a monumental achievement upon which to build.

5 Epistrophy: The Performance of Cultural (Re)Memory in Langston Hughes's *Montage of a Dream Deferred*

HAVING EXAMINED STERLING BROWN'S riffs on vernacular forms, we can now observe the next phase in the development of blues poetics by examining Langston Hughes's *Montage of a Dream Deferred*. Like Brown's *Southern Road, Montage of a Dream Deferred* captures a fighting spirit produced in part by the effects of war. Just as World War I created a labor shortage, World War II caused a vacuum that was filled by black migrants who poured into America's urban centers. Like their counterparts a generation earlier, the migrants of the 1940s sought jobs and the fulfillment of their hopes and dreams. However, life in urban America was far from idyllic. Though the war brought the end of the Depression, tensions were still high. There were riots in Detroit and Harlem in 1943.

This militant spirit, as Eric Lott points out,[1] was reflected in styles that were by-products of the larger hipster culture of the 1940s. Working-class youths donned zoot suits and created their own jargon. Bebop musicians refused to conform to the Satchmo-like image of the grinning entertainer and insisted that audiences treat them as artists. As the drummer Kenny Clarke said, "'There was a message [to black people] in our music. Whatever you go into, go into it intelligently.'"[2] For bebop musicians, musical eloquence and sophistication were most effectively expressed in what Lott calls "an aesthetic of speed and displacement—ostentatious virtuosity dedicated to reorienting perception even as it rocked the house."[3]

The demands for social change that bebop expressed sonically elicited hostile responses from mainstream institutions. Eric Porter notes that the Los Angeles radio station KMPC referred to bebop as "hot jive" and banned it from its airwaves, and *Time* magazine misrepresented the music by deemphasizing its artistic qualities and associating it with drugs, impudent jargon, and suggestive lyrics.[4] That Hughes recognized the political implications of bebop is clear from a passage from "Simple on Bop Music": " 'Everytime a cop hits a Negro with his billy, that old stick says, "BOP! BOP! . . . BE-BOP! . . . MOP! . . . BOP!" And that Negro hollers, "Ooool-ya-koo! Ou-o-o-!" Old cop just beats on, "MOP! MOP! . . . BE-BOP! MOP!" That's where Be-Bop came from, beaten right out of some Negro's head into them horns and saxophones and guitars and piano keys that plays it.' "[5] The statement by Simple suggests that there is a direct relationship between black music and political conditions. As Lionel Hampton has said, " 'Whenever I see any injustice or any unfair action against my own race or any other minority groups Hey Ba Ba Rebop stimulates the desire to destroy such prejudice and discrimination.' "[6]

Yet when he wrote a children's book without the mask of a fictional character, Hughes deemphasized any political underpinnings of bebop: " 'Sometimes for fun, singers sing "oo-ya-koo" to boppish backgrounds today, as Cab Calloway in the 1930s sang "hi-de-hi-de-ho-de-hey," meaning nothing, or as Lionel Hampton sang "hey-baba-re-bop" in 1940, or as Louis Armstrong used to sing "scat" syllables to his music in Chicago in the 1920s, or as Jelly Roll Morton shouted meaningless words to ragtime music in the early 1900s . . . for fun. Nonsense syllables are not new in poetry or music, but they are *fun*.' "[7] Though the contrast between the two statements suggests that Hughes was disingenuous, the word "fun" is an index to the very stuff of blues music. Its incantational quality and its ability to inspire humor in the face of adversity is the basis of its opposition to the status quo. While Hughes appears to have contradicted himself, he actually described two distinct albeit related aspects of the blues idiom.

That bebop informed the fabric of *Montage of a Dream Deferred* is clear from Hughes's prefatory statement: "In terms of current Afro-American popular music and the sources from which it has progressed—jazz, ragtime, swing, blues, boogie-woogie, and be-bop—this poem on contemporary Harlem, like be-bop, is marked by conflicting changes, sudden nuances, sharp and impudent interjections, broken rhythms, and passages sometimes in the manner of the jam session, sometimes the popular song, punctuated by the riffs, runs, breaks, and disc-tortions of the music of a community in transition."[8] But bebop presented a formidable artistic challenge for Hughes. He had already riffed on blues lyrics and the black speaking voice in *The Weary Blues* and *Fine Clothes to the Jew,* and Brown had experimented even further with riffing in *Southern Road.* But since bebop was primarily an instrumental music, Hughes could not transcribe its sound onto the page. Though he believed that music was an important index to the souls of black folk,[9] by 1948 he understood the potential of the montage form to capture the full panorama of African American culture.[10]

Since he was no longer bound by lyrics or voice, Hughes could visually represent the culture of Harlem. The shifting sequences of the montage allowed him to resolve a presumed opposition between visually oriented modern poetics and the black oral tradition. As Craig Hansen Werner has suggested, one can argue that *Montage* is not inconsistent with the principles of imagism in Ezra Pound's doctrinal statement: "'1. Direct treatment of the "thing," whether subjective or objective. 2. To use absolutely no word that does not contribute to the presentation. 3. As regarding rhythm: to compose in the sequence of the musical phrase, not in sequence of a metronome.'"[11] Werner points out that given Pound's emphasis upon musicality, "the absence of any explicit mention of the visual arts . . . would seem to suggest an underlying compatibility between imagism and Afro-American aesthetics."[12] However, like Brown, Hughes theorized modernism in relation to Afro-vernacular culture, improvising upon the specific inscriptions of black aural calligraphers[13] while working within the conventions of the printed page as well as the recording studio.[14] Therefore, while I agree with the thrust of Werner's statement, it is important to understand that blues poets have tended to interpret "musical phras[ing]" differently from imagist poets.

As Pound had done in his *Cantos,* Hughes conceived *Montage* as one long poem comprised of a series of short poems. But like Thelonius Monk's blues approach to the piano, Hughes, in a brilliant performance of cultural (re)-memory, created a vernacular version of modernism to capture a transitional moment in Harlem. *Montage* has been described as a linguistic jam session in which disparate points of view are juxtaposed.[15] However, while it is important to remember the musical aspects of *Montage,* it is equally important to underscore Hughes's visual experiments. I want to suggest that *Montage* should be read as a multifaceted text in which Hughes employs film techniques to simulate the role of a bebop orchestra leader like Billy Eckstine, whose bands included such musicians as Charlie Parker, Dizzy Gillespie, Miles Davis, and Sarah Vaughan.

At times, Hughes performs cultural (re)memory by repeating terms of (re)memory or simulating blues techniques. I call this method of repetition "epistrophy" after Thelonius Monk's classic composition "Epistrophy," which relies heavily upon repetition. But while the term "epistrophy" is related to the Standard English word "epistrophe," which refers to the repetition of strophes, my metaphor, based upon Monk's unconventional ideas (note his spelling of the word), refers more generally to Afro-modernist[16] poetry. Just as Monk conceptualized modernism as a revision of sanctified church music,[17] so Hughes envisioned modernism as a fusion of oral forms and modernist techniques, creating what Art Lange calls "'word pictures.'"[18]

Montage of a Dream Deferred includes fragments of various discourses, including journalistic commentaries, newspaper headlines, commercial advertisements, aphoristic statements, and epistolary writing. In addition, *Montage* includes riffs on vernacular forms, such as African American urban speech (including bebop jargon), ballads, blues, folk rhymes, and bebop itself. At times, Hughes replicates camera shots to create the illusion of actual sites in Harlem. For instance, in "Neon Signs," he repeats the names of several marquees:

MINTON'S
(ancient altar of Thelonius)

.

. .

.

MANDALAY
Spots where the booted
and unbooted play

.

. .

.

SMALL'S[.] (397)

In "125th Street," Hughes employs imagistic techniques to revise stereotypical images and illustrate the beauty of the people:

Face like a chocolate bar
full of nuts and sweet.

Face like a jack-o'-lantern,
candle inside.

Face like a slice of melon,
grin that wide. (407)

Most often, though, Hughes interweaves these forms around the phrase "a dream deferred," which reflects his belief that blacks have been consistently denied opportunities in America. The phrase "a dream deferred" is repeated intermittently throughout *Montage* and functions as a riff chorus for the entire poem. At the same time, Hughes replicates the shifting sequences of the montage to approximate the ab pattern in music. Hence, many poems that evince no formal relationship to the black oral tradition are informed by an internal intertextuality that simulates the call and response method of blues music.

Hughes complements his dream motif by using the American class struggle as a subtext. In "Ballad of the Landlord," he blends film techniques with a riff on the ballad form. Unlike Sterling Brown's riffs on the ballad in *Southern Road*, Hughes's revision is not an attempt to render a mimetic portrayal of the form. Rather, he attempts to convey a sense of the form to readers, so that he could use it unapologetically as a weapon of propaganda like American folk musicians and Hughes himself had done in the 1930s. The ironic title suggests the nature of Hughes's experiment with the ballad. In referring to the landlord, Hughes calls attention to the problem of authorship in cultural politics: From what and/or whose point of view does the public view the opposition between workers and the ruling class? The poem begins with the speaker telling his apartment owner about the rundown condition of his apartment:

Landlord, landlord,
My roof has sprung a leak
Don't you 'member I told you about it
Way last week?

Landlord, landlord,
these steps is broken down.
When you come up yourself
It's a wonder you don't fall down. (402)

Like Brown in "Odyssey of Big Boy," Hughes allows his character to speak for himself to create a more realistic effect than that afforded by the traditional form, wherein the hero's experiences are narrated in the third person. Unlike Brown's poem and the traditional ballads, though, Hughes's ballad is not a narrative of his character's life but rather focuses on a pivotal moment in the life of his character, who is a laboring every(wo)man of sorts.

After demonstrating the legitimacy of the worker's complaint, Hughes cleverly describes the intensity of the owner's determination to maximize his profits. Hughes mediates the owner's reactions to the worker through his responses to the owner. In the process, Hughes exposes the ruling class's strategies of containment. First, the owner uses projection and threatens eviction:

> Ten Bucks you say I owe you?
> Ten Bucks you say is due?
> Well, that's Ten Bucks more'n I'll pay you
> Till you fix this house up new.
>
> What? You gonna get eviction orders?
> You gonna cut off my heat?
> You gonna take my furniture and
> Throw it in the street? (402)

After the worker threatens to "land [his] fist on" the owner, the process of misrepresentation begins:

> Copper's whistle!
> Patrol bell!
> Arrest.
>
> Precinct Station.
> Iron cell.
> Headlines in press:
>
> MAN THREATENS LANDLORD
> .
> . .
>
> TENANT HELD NO BAIL
> .
> . .
>
> JUDGE GIVES NEGRO 90 DAYS IN COUNTY JAIL. (403)

Hughes's shift to visual media is an excellent performance of epistrophy. While many black poets summon cultural (re)memory with allusions, Hughes, like John Dos Passos in his *U.S.A.* trilogy, records the black cultural experience in "Ballad of the Landlord." In so doing, he extends the conventions of traditional ballads. Rather than concluding when the police apprehend the worker, Hughes continues the narrative by replicating camera shots, illustrating the sequence of events. The last line is especially poignant because it repeats countless headlines of similar injustices.

At the same time, "Ballad of the Landlord" also illustrates the mythology inscribed in the notion of individualism. That is, the poem demonstrates that the failure of marginalized groups in America to develop broad coalitions has led to an impotent opposition. Trapped inside a logic that confuses machisimo with radicalism, the speaker resorts to spontaneous violence that is utterly insufficient because the apartment owner is part of a system of individuals who work in concert, if not conspiracy, to thwart not only the tenant's efforts to seek redress but also any attempt to express sympathy for the conditions that precipitated the conflict.

If "Ballad of the Landlord" describes how the dream is deferred, "Projection" reflects Hughes's vision of how to begin the process of realizing the dream:

> On the day when the Savoy
> leaps clean over to Seventh Avenue
> and starts jitterbugging
> with the Renaissance,
> on that day when Abyssinia Baptist Church
> throws her enormous arms around
> St. James Presbyterian[.] (403)

Note the repeated terms of black cultural (re)memory. Hughes uses personification to maximize the effect of his imagery. For instance, the "enormous arms" suggest both the heavyset women in the congregation as well as the influence wielded by the church. The Savoy Ballroom was a historic site for the development of African American performance styles, serving as a musicological laboratory for Charlie Parker, Dizzy Gillespie, Thelonius Monk, and others,[19] and it was the site of Gillespie and Parker's first collaboration.[20] The phrase "Savoy / leaps" recalls the (re)memory of "Lester Leaps In" by the saxophonist Lester Young, an innovative Kansas City stylist who was a forerunner of bebop. More specifically, "Savoy / leaps" recalls the Lindy Hop dance that was performed at the Savoy Ballroom. As the trombonist Dickie Wells recalls, "'I used to watch those Lindy Hoppers throw those women all the way to the roof in the Savoy . . . and grab 'em when they came down. And doing all the stepping, up they go again.'"[21] Similarly, the jitterbug image evokes the dance itself and the percussive rhythms of the bands to which the dancers performed. Hughes uses the term "jitterbugging" as a metaphor for discourse, just as dance commonly serves as a device that facilitates dialogue.

To maximize the effect of his imagery, Hughes employs a riff chorus to

simulate a "jitterbugging" music of his own. As the phrase "On the day" is
repeated with variations, the poem accumulates emotional intensity, which,
in turn, increases the speaker's desire for unification:

> On that day—
> Do, Jesus!
> Manhattan Island will whirl
> like a Dizzy Gillespie transcription[.] (404)

But while *"Peace!"* is *"truly / wonderful,"* Hughes's dream of a unified African
American nation ignores the tremendous problems that many marginalized
groups encounter in their attempts to resist ruling hegemony. As Hughes
himself demonstrates in "Parade," large segments of the black elite can only
envision blackness as a coffee-colored reflection of the colonizer.

In contrast to the folk-based, nationalist construct in "Projection," "Parade" introduces the prospect of unification controlled by the black elite.
The conspicuous lack of references to either boogie-woogie or bebop suggests a (pre)neocolonial vision that rejects the sonic implications of the
blues idiom as well as the radical viewpoint of the worker in "Ballad of the
Landlord":

> Seven ladies
> and seventeen gentlemen
> at the Elks Club Lounge
> planning planning a parade:
> Grand Marshal in his white suit
> will lead it.
> Cadillacs with dignitaries
> will precede it. (388)

The repetition of "planning" suggests the black elite's narcissism and its habit
of ignoring the problems of the downtrodden. The Cadillac and Elks Club
images imply a refusal to question the hegemony of the dominant culture.
Though the black elite embraces the notions of freedom and democracy, this
class can only conceptualize liberation as a quest for material luxury. Note
the title "Grand Marshal," which signifies pomp and grandeur. The mission
of the black elite, we see, is not to change society but rather to become part
of the ruling oligarchy.

The black elite's rejection of blues music does not constitute a rejection
of music per se, but the militarism implied in the regimented steps of the
marching band reflects the group's intolerance of ideological difference.

Hughes relies upon rhyme and repetition to establish his rhythm but does not attempt to recreate the sounds of the band even though marching bands produce their own distinct sounds. Instead, Hughes uses monologue:

And behind will come
with band and drum
on foot . . . on foot . . .
on foot[.] . . . (389)

The band and drum images suggest the instrumental music, and the repeated "foot" image suggests the percussive sounds of the band's steps.

The complexity of the problems intersecting race and class can be observed in the crowd's reaction to the parade. Though the entire affair has been underwritten by bourgeois politics, the procession creates an opportunity for black collectivity. As a result, it stimulates nationalist sentiments and has an electric effect on the crowd:

I never knew
that many Negroes
were on earth,
did you?

I never knew!

    PARADE!

A chance to let

    PARADE!

the whole world see

    PARADE!

old black me! (389)

Hughes employs a method he introduced in 1926 in "The Cat and the Saxophone (2 A.M.)," in which he juxtaposes a dialogue between two lovers against the lyrics of a blues song. Here, as is in "Dead in There," Hughes uses short lines and stanzas to create a parade image by simulating film techniques. He further attempts to affect his readers visually by juxtaposing the parade image against a monologue.

Hughes again explores the intersection of race and class in "Low to High" and "High to Low." In the former poem, Hughes riffs on the black urban voice and creates a character who presents a call to the more affluent segment of Harlem:

How can you forget me?
But you do!
You said you was gonna take me
Up with you—
Now you've got your Cadillac,
you done forgot that you are black.
How can you forget me
When I'm you? (411)

The passage is characteristic of epistrophy. Hughes infuses just enough of the traditional blues stanza to lend credibility to the speaker's painful sense of betrayal by the black middle class. Note the repetition of the first line as well as the rhyme that ends lines five and six. The Cadillac signifies the luxury attained in part by constructing identities based upon an attempt to mirror the dominant culture and to deemphasize any cultural connections to an African past.

"High to Low" is a response to "Low to High." Not surprisingly, there is no mention of racism, yet the speaker suggests that the black working class has no monopoly on experiences of victimization. In a manner that typifies the confusion of the black elite, the speaker mistakenly blames black workers for the problems that middle-class blacks encounter in their attempts to climb the American social ladder. The luxuries and relative economic security have produced a sense of arrogance that renders the speaker myopic to the implicit wisdom inscribed within the African American working-class sensibility:

One trouble is you:
you talk too loud,
cuss too loud,
look too black,
[. . .]
the way you shout out loud in church,
(not St. Philip's)
and the way you lounge on doorsteps
just as if you were down South,
(not at 409)
the way you clown—
[. . .]
me, trying to uphold the race[.] (411–12)

The ironic point of view arouses humor and facilitates Hughes's description of the speaker's ludicrous worldview. Note the repetition of the word "loud." The speaker is referring not only to noise. He is suggesting that the former speaker's very style of life is ugly and worthy of censure simply because of its departure from the American norm—even though black workers have been thwarted in their attempts to live a "normal" lifestyle. Though the poem is humorous, it is important to understand the absurdity of the speaker's vision. After the Harlem riot in 1943, many "Sugar Hill" blacks expressed disapproval because they felt that the riot deterred social mobility.[22]

The sensibility that produced the "loud" and raucous behavior of southern blacks evolved in America's urban centers. The veneer of obsequiousness that was necessary for survival in the rural South had little utility in the cities. Stoicism gave way to hipness. And yet the riddle of the zoot suit[23] presented quite a problem for mid-century black writers. Ralph Ellison analyzed hipster style and behavior in *Invisible Man,* but otherwise the hipster was largely ignored. Like Ellison, Hughes also understood the radical politics that were implicit in the hipster's zoot suit and language. In his famous poem "Motto," Hughes focuses on the hip new language and riffs on it to illustrate its beauty and describe the worldview associated with it:

I play it cool
And dig all jive.
That's the reason
I stay alive.

My motto,
As I live and learn,
   is:
Dig And Be Dug
In Return. (398)

While "Motto" is seemingly innocuous, it is as oppositional as "White Man," a 1930s poem wherein the speaker asks the "White Man," "Is your name in a book / Called the *Communist Manifesto?*" (195). The speaker in "Motto" abides by a code of morality that is diametrically opposed to the constraints that the dominant class wishes to impose upon him. Since "cool[ness]" denotes tolerance, that is, the ability to "dig all jive," the moral code that is inscribed in the word "cool" constitutes a rebellion against exclusion.

At the same time, Hughes demonstrates that there are grave consequences to rebellion. In "Dead in There," the counterpoint to "Motto," Hughes uses typography and elegiac imagery to describe a funeral:

Sometimes
A night funeral
Going by
Carries home
A cool bop daddy.

Hearse and flowers
Guarantee
He'll never hype
Another paddy.

It's hard to believe,
But dead in there,
He'll never lay a
Hype nowhere! (399)

The short lines and stanzas accentuate the illusion of a funeral by simulating a camera shot. But while the late hipster receives a burial, it is noteworthy that his epitaphist is not a preacher but rather a fellow hipster. The term "cool" is ironic in that it refers both to his death and to the hipster's lifestyle that was based upon "hyp[ing] / padd[ies]," that is, hustling whites out of money.

In "Children's Rhymes," Hughes uses dialogue between an older adult and children to describe the rift between the two generations and thereby provide a more in-depth depiction of the social tranformations in Harlem. But whereas the militancy of the hipsters is merely implied in "Motto," the speakers in "Children's Rhymes" openly express a radical politics that they perceive in the hipster's attitude toward America's Herrenvolk democracy:

When I was a chile we used to play,
"One—two—buckle my shoe!"
and things like that. But now, Lord,
listen at them little varmints! (390)

The passage reflects a recurrent theme related to Hughes's dream deferral motif: aural calligraphy has served as a psychological device with which blacks have responded to marginalization. Like Brown, Hughes believed that Afro-vernacular culture inscribed a style of life that called into question the privileged position of the dominant culture as a naturalized construct. The irony, of course, is that the older speaker, whose speech attests to his participation in that culture, expresses frustration at the children's ability to question the hegemony of Anglo-American narratives and create their own forms to confront the realities of their own era.

By what sends
the white kids
I ain't sent:
I know I can't
be President. (390)

As the poem progresses, the rhymes become more militant:

> *What's written down*
> *for white folks*
> *ain't for us a-tall:*
> *"Liberty And Justice—*
> *Huh—For All."*
>
> *Oop-pop-a-da!*
> *Skee! Daddle-de-do!*
> *Be-bop!*
>
> Salt' peanuts
>
> De-dop! (390)

The resentment toward the hypocrisy of racial discrimination notwithstanding, the passage is a testimony to the agency inscribed in African American orature[24] and its capacity to evolve dialogically vis-à-vis specific historical conditions, providing creative outlets for emotions and ideas that cannot be expressed in officially sanctioned institutions like school and church.

The bop passage is equally effective in sound and print and contitutes an excellent performance of cultural (re)memory. While the passage reads as an onomatopoeic illustration of urban vernacular, it is notable that "Salt Peanuts" and "Oop-pop-a-da" were among Dizzy Gillespie's earliest recordings. Gillespie later recorded "Ooop-pop-a-da" with the Cuban conga player Chano Pozo and demonstrated the internationalism implicit in the blues idiom.

Hughes's political identification with black workers is also reflected in poems that riff on blues stanzas. Though none of the poems in *Montage* strictly follows the traditional three-line aab stanzaic pattern of the twelve-bar blues, "Blues at Dawn" bears a close resemblance. However, the poem is not a riff on the country blues songs that inspired Brown but an illustration of the revised blues songs of the big city. "Blues at Dawn" actually has an aaba pattern. But like Brown in "Southern Road," Hughes breaks the third line in half to lend more aural power to its rhyme in scripted form:

> I don't dare remember in the morning.
> Don't dare remember in the morning.
> > If I recall the day before,
> > I wouldn't get up no more—
> So I don't dare remember in the morning. (420)

Although Hughes is effective in evoking a blues mood, one should note the language here. There are no apostrophes to suggest the southern black voice. Also, the word "recall" (as opposed to "recollect") is a term that would not be commonly used in country blues lyrics.

In "Same in Blues," Hughes employs four-line stanzas with abcb rhyme schemes to simulate a jazz quintet. Each stanza is an expression of a distinct voice, so that the poem approximates the personal nature of the blues idiom and the capacity of the music to accommodate individual expression in a communal context. As the title suggests, "Same in Blues" describes the psychological impact of the dream deferral upon black workers by providing fragments of dialogues that illustrate how various people have been affected. Note the italicized passages that serve as a rhetorical basis for the dialogues that are interwoven around it:

> I said to my baby,
> Baby, take it slow.
> I can't, she said, I can't!
> I got to go!
>
> > *There's a certain*
> > *amount of traveling*
> > *in a dream deferred.*
>
> Lulu said to Leonard,
> I want a diamond ring.
> Leonard said to Lulu,
> You won't get a goddamn thing!
>
> > *A certain*
> > *amount of nothing*
> > *in a dream deferred.* (427)

Hughes's best performance of epistrophy is perhaps illustrated in his "boogie" poems as well as the poems that serve as a call and/or response to them. As Stephen Tracy has pointed out, the term "boogie" refers to a specific dance step.[25] However, the term can also refer not only to dancing but to travel as well. According to Tracy, Hughes's six "boogie" poems are composed around a boogie-woogie beat. However, I want to argue that, in the most aural "boogie" poems, Hughes incorporates the boogie-woogie beat within a larger jazz aesthetic to simulate a hybrid musical form. "Dream Boogie," the first poem in the series, provides a good example of how Hughes replicates the synthesizing formula of blues music. Hughes's simulation of hybridization in "Dream Boogie" constitutes a formal approximation of the reconstructive project that he felt was necessary in real life. Boogie-woogie was primarily a music of piano and vocals. Pianists like Pete Johnson and Cow Cow Davenport and blues singers like Lonnie Johnson and Memphis Slim created an urban blues style that appealed strongly to newly arrived southerners.[26] In his own "boogie" performance, Hughes reconnects two divergent strands of the blues impulse by combining boogie-woogie images with bebop images, while replicating a bebop rhythm:

> Good morning, daddy!
> Ain't you heard
> The boogie-woogie rumble
> Of a dream deferred?
>
> Listen closely:
> You'll hear their feet
> Beating out and beating out a—[.] (388)

The first stanza functions as a riff chorus that is repeated with variations throughout *Montage.* This is a particularly effective device because it inscribes within the structure of the poem the repeated denials of opportunity to African Americans. Hughes employs the riff chorus here just as jazz bands begin their tunes with a riff chorus. The dash functions like a break in jazz. The expected word, "beat," is not mentioned. Instead, another speaker interjects a question: *"You think / It's a happy beat?"* The implication, of course, is that the gaiety of black dance is a dialogic response to their harsh living conditions:

> Listen to it closely:
> Ain't you heard
> something underneath
> like a—
>
> *What did I say?* (388)

Here the riff chorus, repeated with a variation, establishes a basis for another break that is signified again by the dash. This time the expected word is "rumble," which implies the brooding sentiments lurking beneath the surface.

It is also noteworthy that the dialogue between the two speakers functions like a duet. It is ironic, though, that the main speaker, who has called attention to the repressed anger, responds: "Sure, / I'm happy! / Take it away!" (388). And the second speaker complies:

> *Hey, pop!*
> *Re-bop!*
> *Mop!*
>
> *Y-e-a-h!* (388)

The speaker is a skillful interpreter of music; he or she grasps its subtle nuances, which makes it possible to discern the submerged anger that is suggested rhythmically. Nonetheless, sophisticated musical ideas do not necessarily lead to political consciousness.

Thus, Hughes points out the sharp discrepancy between the political implications of Afro-vernacular culture and concrete political realities. The speaker's refusal to answer the question directly indicates that his or hers is an emotive revolt. The music does not aim to change the political landscape; the "boogie-woogie rumble" is directed at an interior space in which an alternative sensibility can be developed.

The next "boogie" poem, "Easy Boogie," is framed by "Wonder" and "Movies." Hughes plays the images of each poem contrapuntally to simulate an antiphonal effect. First, he replicates a camera shot in "Wonder" to capture the topography of nighttime Harlem:

> Early blue evening.
> Lights ain't come on yet.
> *Looky yonder!*
> *They come on now!* (394)

The combination of the "blue evening," light images, and the speaker's announcement sets the stage, as it were, for "Easy Boogie." After the speaker says, "*They come on now!*" Hughes replicates a live performance of blues music. He does not, as in "Weary Blues," attempt to riff on the lyrics that accompanied boogie-woogie pianists. Like the musicians who improvise upon the twelve-bar blues form, Hughes elaborates upon the aab stanzaic structure. But whereas blues stanzas usually consist of three lines with four bars each, Hughes composes three four-line stanzas:

> Down in the bass
> That steady beat
> Walking walking walking
> Like marching feet.
>
> Down in the bass
> That easy roll,
> Rolling like I like it
> In my soul.
>
>   Riffs, smears, breaks.
>
> Hey, Lawdy, Mama!
> Do you hear what I said?

Easy like I rock it
In my bed! (395)

All three stanzas have the same abcb rhyme scheme. The first stanza establishes the call; the second stanza is both a variation of the first and a response to it; and the third stanza is a clear expression of the implicit statements in the first two stanzas.

In its self-reflexive representation of blues instrumental music, "Easy Boogie" anticipates Jayne Cortez's "In the Morning." "Easy Boogie" describes the dynamics of African American performance within a specific historical and artistic context. The phrase "Riffs, smears, breaks" approximates a break in jazz, and the walking bass image summons the (re)memory of the innovations in the rhythm sections of bebop bands. The repetition of the first lines in the first two stanzas is an artifice to lure readers into anticipating a repetition of the previous stanza. But as in "Dream Boogie," Hughes frustrates the reader's expectations and shifts the focus to describe an audience member's emotional reaction to the music.

Part of the reason that blues music serves as a tonic against resignation is its incantational quality. In "Easy Boogie," Hughes describes blues instrumentalists' ability to convey sonically what the following blues lyrics express in words: "'What makes my grandma love my grandpa so / S'what makes my grandma love my grandpa so / W' he can still hoochie coochie like he did fifty years ago!'"[27] The word "rock" in the last stanza is a term of (re)memory. Hughes uses the word as a metaphor for sexual intercourse, just as blues singers begin verses with well-known blues lines like, "Rock me baby, rock me all night long."

Hughes contrasts the soulful blues performance with the artificiality of Hollywood in "Movies." While the speaker in "Easy Boogie" is an informed auditor of blues performances, he and other blacks do not understand the conventions of Hollywood films:

Harlem laughing in all the wrong places
    at the crocodile tears
    of crocodile art
    that you know
    in your heart
    is crocodile[.] (395)

The repetition of the "crocodile" cliché reinforces Hughes's belief that Hollywood committed psychological violence against black viewers.

"Boogie: 1 A.M." functions as a coda for "Low to High" in that it depicts black working-class culture away from the workplace and the auditorium. The title calls attention to the percussive dance-beat rhythms that boogie-woogie pianists played. As Amiri Baraka notes, as the main attractions at blue-light, all-night pay-parties that began at one o'clock, the pianists enjoyed sumptuous plates of food at no cost. Depending upon the speciality of the host, party goers could enjoy, in addition to cake and/or ice cream, a main entree of soul food, such as fried fish, chitterlings, hog maws, or gumbo.[28]

As in "Easy Boogie," Hughes revises the denotation of "boogie" to include bebop by focusing upon a jazz rhythm section and describing its capacity to "boogie." But unlike the first two "boogie" poems, in "Boogie: 1 A.M." Hughes does not present a musicopoetic replication of blues music. Rather, he employs compressed imagery after the riff chorus:

> Good evening, daddy!
> I know you've heard
> The boogie-woogie rumble
> Of a dream deferred
> Trilling the treble
> And twining the bass
> Into midnight ruffles
> Of cat-gut lace. (411)

Having already replicated the sound of the walking bass in "Easy Boogie," here Hughes uses a "twining" image, combined with the alliteration of /t/ sounds, to suggest the thumping of the bass. The word "Trilling," which denotes alteration, implies antiphonal percussive sounds. Hughes contrasts the low note suggested by the "twining" bass image with the soprano sounds suggested by the "treble" to approximate an improvisation of his own blues performance within the larger blues modality of *Montage* itself.

As Tracy has argued,[29] the lace and ruffle images operate on a dual level. On the one hand, they suggest the trimmings of the people's Saturday-night attire. On the other hand, "lace" and "ruffle" are both verbs: "lace" denotes binding; "ruffle" denotes disturbance. As in "Dream Boogie," Hughes suggests that there is turmoil lurking beneath the surface. The fine clothes and mouth-watering food mask a "gut"-level reality that the "cat[s]," that is, the people, feel but do not understand. Their response is to dance through the wee hours of the morning to alleviate their pain.

In "Lady's Boogie," which is a counterpart to "Boogie: 1 A.M.," Hughes shifts the focus to a middle-class black woman. Just as "Boogie: 1 A.M." illustrates the psychology of black working-class culture, so "Lady's Boogie" describes the false consciousness of a Sugar Hill black woman whose world-view complements the comments expressed in "High to Low." Unlike "High to Low," though, the speaker in "Lady's Boogie" is a member of the working class who criticizes a woman's cultural politics:

> See that lady
> Dressed so fine?
> She ain't got boogie-woogie
> On her mind—
>
> But if she was to listen
> I bet she'd hear,
> Way up in the treble
> The tingle of a tear.
>
>   *Be-Bach!* (412)

The speaker's language contrasts with the woman's prim and proper image. The term "fine" and the incorrect subjunctive demonstrate his or her lack of formal education. But as a product of blues culture, the speaker has developed a sharp sense of wit. His or her ironic bebop pun constitutes, in jazz lexicon, a signifying riff that is directed at the "lady" and others who share her snobbish attitude.

Notwithstanding the humor, however, the poem is actually an appeal to middle-class blacks to challenge their presumptions about African American identity. Hughes suggests that the "lady's" antipathy toward boogie-woogie stems from her reluctance to experience—even vicariously—the pain associated with working-class black life. As a skilled listener, the speaker is aware that if well-to-do blacks really "listen[ed]" to boogie-woogie music, they would hear "[t]he tingle of a tear." Yet they cannot because they can only conceptualize African American subjectivity in terms of the dominant culture, albeit a coffee-colored version: hence, the reference to Bach.

The psychological impact of living in a society in which race is a metaphor for class oppression can be observed in "Nightmare Boogie," which is a response to "Passing." "Passing" is, of course, a term of black cultural (re)-memory and recalls a history of light-skinned blacks who have lied about their racial identity so that they may live as whites. Here Hughes repeats the title of Nella Larsen's novel, *Passing,* and revises the traditional meaning to refer to elite blacks "who've crossed the line / to live downtown" (417).

After "Passing," Hughes penetrates the persona's psyche in "Nightmare Boogie," wherein he responds contrapuntally:

I had a dream
and I could see
a million faces
black as me!
A nightmare dream:
Quicker than light
All them faces
turned dead white!
Boogie-woogie,
Rolling bass,
Whirling treble
of cat-gut lace. (418)

Here Hughes illustrates the blues idiom's dialectical position vis-à-vis the dominant ideology. The politics of race and class converge in "Nightmare Boogie" to render invisible the black labor base that sustains international capitalist hegemony: "*All them faces / turned dead white!*" But the hallmark of the blues is that it resists such invisiblity, insisting that the black presence be affirmed via sonic representations of everyday black life. In linking caste and class in American society, Hughes questions class privilege as a natural-ized phenomenon and suggests that such privilege is the consequence of an economic-political apparatus. Where the dominant culture projects a lily-white image of America as the norm, the blues speaker reads ubiquitous whiteness as a nightmare. Insofar as blacks have had access to social mobil-ity, they have largely been forced to deny their own cultural memory. Hence, the death image as an ostensible reference to skin color notwithstanding, the image more fundamentally describes the persona's sense of dejection. The boogie-woogie images, then, suggest the medicinal qualities of the music, which enables blacks to cope with the nightmare of white America.

"Dream Boogie: Variation" and "Hope" comprise the final pieces of the call-and-response pattern in the "boogie" series. In "Hope," Hughes focuses on an elderly couple; the ironic title calls attention to their utter despair. Their poverty has compelled them to grapple with the contradictions be-tween their hopes and the stark reality of their lives:

He rose up on his dying bed
and asked for fish.
His wife looked it up in her dream book
and played it. (425)

Note the lack of grief. Rather than preparing for a funeral, the woman views her husband's death as a good omen and attempts to exploit his death by gambling.

Like his artistic models, who improvise upon a given musical theme, Hughes elaborates upon the graphic scene in "Hope." As the title suggests (note the similarity between "Hope" and "Dream"), Hughes shifts the focus to a boogie-woogie pianist who performs a musical interpretation of the image in "Hope." There is no hint of bop here. The boogie-woogie pianist performs solo, and his music suggests neither dance nor sexuality—only pain from the dream deferred:

> Tinkling treble
> Rolling bass,
> High noon teeth
> In a midnight face,
> Great long fingers
> On great big hands,
> Screaming pedals
> Where his twelve-shoe lands,
> Looks like his eyes
> Are teasing pain,
> A few minutes late
> For the Freedom Train. (425–26)

The pianist's physical features recall a long history of misrepresentation. But as in "125th Street," Hughes revises the Sambo image. Whereas ideology de-historicizes colonized peoples, Hughes's conclusion calls attention to America's history of slavery and segregation. The train metaphor is particularly effective. It invokes blues musicians' fascination with trains, replicating their sounds instrumentally. Hughes points up the tension of the situation in the contrast between the movement suggested by the train image and the lack of social mobility afforded to blacks.

Given the painful depictions of the dream deferral in "Hope" and "Dream Boogie: Variation," one might expect Hughes to lighten the tone of *Montage*. However, in the next poem, "Harlem," he presents an imagistic illustration that complements the previous two poems:

> What happens to a dream deferred?
>
>> Does it dry up
>> like a raisin in the sun?
>> Or fester like a sore—
>> And then run?
>> Does it stink like rotten meat? (426)

Observe the precision of the imagery. The raisin metaphor suggests black people's skin color, their history of toiling long hours under "ol hannah," and also the whip-scarred backs of the slaves who dared to resist the codes of slavery. The sore image calls attention to the indifference to the pain that African Americans have endured. And the rotten meat metaphor reminds readers of the squalid conditions in which blacks have been forced to live.

In his conclusion, Hughes responds to the question that opens the poem: "Maybe it just sags / like a heavy load. / / *Or does it explode?*" (426). The explosion reflects Hughes's belief that America would continue to be plagued by riots until blacks receive justice. Thus, he prophetically predicts the mass-scale violence that would erupt in the 1960s and anticipates Haki Madhubuti's "But He Was Cool." Hughes reinforces the effectiveness of his imagery with typographical experiments. By shaping the poem like an inverted missile, Hughes suggests that racial discrimination is comparable to a ticking time bomb. The length of the first line suggests a base. The separation of the second and third stanzas creates the illusion of a tip, and the italics accent the force of the explosion.

But while Hughes presaged the violence of the 1960s, he understood that such mass resistance was not imminent in the late 1940s. Though some of the Harlemites understood that "the trains are late" and that "there're bars / at each gate" (427), many of the migrants were concerned primarily with economic survival. In "Letter," Hughes riffs on African American epistolary writing to illustrate the naiveté of many new migrants:

> *Dear Mama,*
>   *Time I pay rent and get my food*
> *and laundry I don't have much left*
> *but here is five dollars for you*
> *to show you I still appreciates you.*
> *My girl-friend send her love and say*
> *she hopes to lay eyes on you sometime in life.*
> *Mama, it has been raining cats and dogs up*
> *here. Well, that is all so I will close.*
>   *Your son baby*
>   *Respectably as ever,*
>   *Joe[.]* (429)

"Letter" can be read as a black counterpart to W. H. Auden's "Unknown Citizen." Joe understands that he has not attained the dream, yet unlike the worker in "Ballad of the Landlord," he continues to believe in it. The irony of the poem lies in the contrast between Joe's patience and the reader's aware-ness of the futility of his efforts to escape poverty.

The critical neglect of *Montage of a Dream Deferred* by critics of African American literature constitutes an omission of singular magnitude. Like Margaret Walker and Robert Hayden, Hughes addresses the tension between the black oral tradition and modern literary conventions. However, the pub-lication of *Montage* prefigured Sherley Anne Williams's *Some One Sweet Angel Chile* and foreshadowed the beginning of a "pre-future"[30] form in African American poetry because it allowed Hughes to explore the possibil-ities of revising the notion of the poetic artifact.

It is not extraordinary that Hughes recorded much of *Montage* on an album entitled *Weary Blues*. Beat poets such as Kenneth Rexroth, Lawrence Ferlinghetti, and Bob Kaufman gained popularity from poetry readings with jazz in the 1950s. But when Hughes collaborated with the bassist Charles Mingus, a major innovator of bebop music who composed and shaped ma-terial for the album,[31] the two artists fused black oral and aural expressions and anticipated Kalamu ya Salaam's album *My Story, My Song* and Jayne Cortez's performances with her own band.

6　　Taking the Blues Back Home:
　　　The Incarnation of Secular Priesthood
　　　in the Poetry of Jayne Cortez

WHEN THE HARPIST ALICE COLTRANE joined John Coltrane's band as a pianist, it was an important historical moment for black women musicians. Like Lil Hardin and Mary Lou Williams generations earlier, Coltrane's achievements helped pave the way for contemporary women musicians like the pianist Gerri Allen and the drummer Terri Lyne Carrington. While women had always been in the forefront of blues music as vocalists, few had opportunities to excel as instrumentalists. Yet Coltrane was unique in that she became a virtuoso on the harp, which is still rarely featured in jazz bands today. Similarly, Jayne Cortez has achieved success in a male-dominated art form. Of course, Nikki Giovanni and Sonia Sanchez were two of the most popular poets in the Black Arts Movement. But the tendency to define resistance in terms of violence privileged male poets who sometimes implied that revolution was as imminent as the next thunderstorm.

Cortez was undaunted. Like the activists Fannie Lou Hamer, Angela Davis, and the Black Panther leader Elaine Brown, she was determined to disrupt traditional assumptions about gender in political movements, and she forged her poetry in the flames of struggle. Her first book, *Pisstained Stairs and the Monkey Man's Wares,* was published during the height of the

Black Power movement in 1969. A year earlier, Martin Luther King was assasinated, and a seventeen-year-old Black Panther member, Bobby Hutton, was killed in a shoot-out with Oakland police. Cortez's poetry reflects the revolutionary spirit of this period and demonstrates her political commitment to resist colonization on an international scale.

Cortez's poetry demonstrates the full potential of blues poetics. Having examined riffing and the performance of cultural (re)memory, we are now prepared to observe how both methods can be utilized when a poet incarnates the blues musician. Cortez's development as a poet seems to coincide with the development of an internationalist worldview and an interest in surrealism, the radical politics of which are compatible with the ideas of Black Arts theorists. André Breton believed that artists and intellectuals should identify with workers, and his idea of igniting resistive energy by plunging into the depths of one's interior resembles Haki Madhubuti's emphasis upon political consciousness in "a poem to complement other poems."[1] It also recalls the Negritude poet Aime Cesaire's statement: "Surrealism interested me to the extent that it was a liberating factor."[2] As Aldon Lynn Nielsen has pointed out, even though some surrealists were themselves racists, their 1933 statement in Nancy Cunard's *Negro,* "With [the white man's] psalms, his speeches, his guarantees of liberty, equality, and fraternity, he seeks to drown the noise of his machine guns," prefigures much of Black Arts poetry.[3] Though André Breton mistakenly assumed that all artists are products of the bourgeoisie, surrealists were committed to a "tenet of revolt, complete insubordination [and] sabotage according to rule."[4] In addition, surrealists displayed an awareness of class oppression. Breton states: "It is up to [the poetry specialists and art critics] . . . to move, as slowly as necessary . . . toward the worker's way of thinking."[5]

In its rejection of simplistic either/or oppositions, surrealism has allowed Cortez to fully realize Larry Neal's dream of a people's poetry. The critical neglect of her work by Black Arts critics calls attention to the irony of Cortez's artistic achievement.[6] While the nationalist vision of many Black Arts poets restricted their attention to African American cultural forms, Cortez's interest in surrealism is analogous to blues musicians' fascination with Western instruments. Just as black musicians discovered that they could create the effects they desired by applying oral techniques to Western instruments, so Cortez has employed surrealism to enhance her blues aesthetic: hence, her fourth book is entitled *Mouth on Paper.*[7]

More specifically, Cortez's poetic style exemplifies blues music's propensity for creolization in that it blends surrealistic imagery with rhythms that usually riff on the black sermon form. Moreover, in establishing her own band with which she performs regularly, Cortez extends the musico-poetry tradition initiated by Langston Hughes. That is, she blurs the distinctions between poetry and song by literally using her voice as an instrument, often employing vocal techniques that replicate those of blues singers and/or instrumentalists.

Cortez's experiments with blues music and surrealism have created a unique version of an incarnation of secular priesthood wherein her poetry bears a striking resemblance to black sermons, which deserve brief commentary here. Though the black church community has traditionally frowned upon blues music, it has not been uncommon for blues musicians to use church music as a basis for improvisation. Robert Johnson, for instance, wrote and sang a song entitled "Preachin Blues";[8] Bessie Smith sang "Preachin' the Blues";[9] and the pianist Bobby Timmons's "Moanin',"[10] which revises gospel music, is now considered a jazz classic. Similarly, the riff chorus that is employed in the call and response by black preachers and their congregations is a prominent feature in Cortez's poetry and is usually employed as a variation of what Gerald Davis has called a formula set that "develop[s] from a key word, idea, or phrase in the lines immediately preceding the set."[11] For "set" read "riff chorus." Observe the following lines that Davis cites:

> "Churches everywhere
> Churches in the basements
> Churches on the street corner
> Churches in the storefronts and in the garages
> Churches in the dwelling house and
> Churches in the synagogues
> Churches everywhere
> Churches on the air twenty-four hours a day
> Turn on the air and you'll hear somebody preaching Church."[12]

The key word here is, of course, "Churches," and the line "Churches everywhere" concurrently establishes rhythmic and rhetorical bases for subsequent lines.

At times, though, Cortez's key word or phrase is less obvious to readers. Nor does she always convert her key word or phrase into a riff chorus. In "For the Brave Young Students of Soweto," for instance, the riff chorus contributes more to the rhetorical import of the poem than its rhythm. Cortez celebrates the 1976 uprising by South African students by cataloging a series of images that function like a collage to describe the degradation of colonization. At issue was the politics of language. Students marched to protest the government's order that Afrikaans be used as the language of instruction in the schools. After the police killed thirteen-year-old Hector Petersen by shooting him from behind, students rioted, boycotted and burned schools, and attacked police stations and the homes of black policemen.[13]

In the recorded version, the poem is introduced by a duet between the muzette player Bill Cole and the drummer Denardo Coleman, Cortez's son.[14] As the tempo of the drumming increases, the muzette fades, allowing for a brief drum solo before Cortez interjects with her own voice, using the line "when i hear your name" or a variation of it as her key phrase to draw parallels between between various colonized groups. First, she implies a political interconnection between South Africans and African Americans:

Soweto
when i hear your name
I think about you
like the fifth ward in Houston Texas[.][15]

Then she focuses on nonblack colonized peoples to emphasize the global nature of colonization:

When i look at this ugliness
and think about the Native Americans pushed
into the famine of tribal reserves
think about the concentration camps full of sad Palestinians[.] (44)

Unlike most Black Arts poets, Cortez does not describe racial hatred as the fundamental problem that colonized people face. Rather, she presents racism as a by-product of capitalism. And she points out that workers in all capitalist societies are forced to perform the most difficult labor but are deprived of the wealth that it produces. She envisions

two black hunters walking into the fire of Sharpeville
into the sweat and stink of gold mines
into your children's eyes suffering from malnutrition
while pellets of uranium are loaded onto boats
headed for France for Israel for Japan[.] (44)

The first line functions as a basis for rhetorical and rhythmic elaboration. In the succeeding lines, Cortez omits the phrase "two black hunters walking" and maintains the image by repeating the word "into" at the beginning of the lines. The reference to Sharpeville, where South African casualties numbered approximately 250, including seventy killed,[16] introduces the theme of violence that is developed later in the poem. Cortez's reference to Japan reflects the complexity of her vision. Although the Japanese have suffered from the devastation of the atom bomb, Cortez understands their role as economic imperialists.

The profits accumulated by the labor of the workers are used to develop and maintain policies and strategies that reify ruling-class privilege. At the same time, however, Cortez illustrates a major distinction between class oppression and the conditions of darker-skinned workers in colonized situations. Whereas white workers suffer from problems created by economics and ideology, colonized workers must also deal with the horror of violence and the construction of mythologies that project savagery onto the colonized. It is apt, then, that Cortez employs the cataloging technique used in black slave seculars to describe the violence that undergirds the marginalization of colonized peoples. Observe Cortez's use of the word "and" to link her lines together:

> away from the river so full of skulls
> and Robben Island so swollen with warriors
> [. . .]
> and i think about the assembly line of dead "Hottentots"
> and the jugular veins of Allende
> and once again how the coffin is divided into dry ink
> how the factory moves like a white cane
> like a volley of bullets in the head of Lummumba
> and death is a death-life held together by shacks
> by widows who cry with their nipples pulled out
> by men who shake with electrodes on the tongue[.] (44)

Although Africans have been stereotyped as bloodthirsty savages, Cortez uses the skull image and the references to the murders of Salvadore Allende and Patrice Lumumba to subvert the imposed image and thereby expose the ruthless exploitation underlying the construction of "black savagery" by colonial regimes. The torture images in the last two lines also reflect the effects of white supremacist mythology, recalling the battle-royal scene in Ralph Ellison's *Invisible Man,* in which the nameless narrator and other black youths who are commanded to lunge for counterfeit money shake "like wet rats" because "the rug was electrified."[17] The Hottentot image is particularly evocative because, in contrast to the views of many peoples in the African Diaspora, steatopygia has been tectonically transformed into an object of ideological assault upon black women. Historically, the term recalls the exploitation of Saartjie (Sarah) Baartman, a South African woman who was taken to Europe during the nineteenth century and paid to exhibit her body in public display as the Hottentot Venus because of her relatively large genitalia, breasts, and buttocks.[18] In Cortez's text, the quotation marks signify not only the misrepresentation of the black female body but also the employment of bourgeois ideology to naturalize the exploitation of black female workers.

The fragmentation that occurs among disfranchised groups is part of the process of colonization. While there are always differences between distinct elements of a given group, privileged groups in (neo)colonial situations are able to exploit the tensions between elements of the colonized while simultaneously forming coalitions among themselves vis-à-vis the (neo)colonizers. Given the apparent futility of open resistance for fear of violence, the people are

> forced into fighting each other
> over a funky job in the sewers of Johannesburg
> divided into labor camps
> fighting over damaged meat and stale bread in
> Harlem divided into factions fighting to keep from fighting
> the ferocious men who are shooting
> into the heads of our small children[.] (45)

Cortez's repetition of the words "divided" and "fighting" reflects her belief that marginalized groups can achieve liberation only through reconstructive efforts that ultimately lead to organized armed resistance. The sewer and decayed food images in Johannesburg and Harlem, respectively, imply not only similar mistreatment but also a common enemy.

Cortez suggests that while the students were specifically opposing the South African government, they were also attacking worldwide oppression. Note the key phrases "to see you" and "when i see you":

> to see you stand on the national bank of America
> like monumental sculpture made of stained bullets
> to see you stand empty handed
> your shoulders open to the world
> each day young blood falling on the earth
> to see you stand in the armed struggle
> next to Mozambique, Angola, Namibia, Zimbabwe
> Soweto i tell you Soweto

when i see you standing up like this
i think about all the forces in the world
confronted by the terrifying rhythms of young students
by their sacrifices
and the revelation that it won't be long now
before everything
in this world changes[.] (46–47)

Cortez does not engage in tonal semantics in "For the Brave Young Students in Soweto." Instead, she relies upon the rhythmic structure of the poem and the blending of her own voice with the members of her band to compel the listener's attention. However, in "U.S./Nigerian Relations," a revised title from the printed version in *Firespitter* entitled "Nigerian/American Relations,"[19] Cortez demonstrates the complexity of sound-based poetics. Although the printed version reads as a simplistic example of prose that is nothing more than a compound sentence, Cortez's performance on the recording is a classic example of the incarnation of secular priesthood.

As is suggested by its title, "U.S./Nigerian Relations" addresses the contradictions of (neo)colonialism. Whereas Africans have been the primary resources for exportation in the past, Cortez suggests that the development of capitalism has caused a reversal. Now the preferred raw materials are minerals that can be refined or converted into products that, in turn, sustain a lifestyle of relative ease. This phenomenon has deprived many Third World peoples of opportunities to acquire meaningful labor in their own countries. Consequently, they feel compelled to migrate to more affluent geographical locations where they are often treated with scorn. Hence, Cortez says,

They want the oil
But they don't want the people
They want the oil
But they don't want the people
They want the oil
But they don't want the people
They want the oil
But they don't want the people
They want the oil
But they don't want the people[.] (26)

The poem is an extended riff chorus. At the outset of the poem, Cortez's lines, which are barely audible at this point in the recorded version, are accented by single drumbeats. As she increases the volume of her voice, the other band members begin to play. When Cortez speeds up the tempo, the band responds, and they all proceed at feverish pace before a brief interlude, when the band plays ensemble without Cortez.

When Cortez returns, she uses an antiphonal approach, alternating the pitch of her voice by enunciating the line "They want the oil" in her speaking voice and enunciating the word "people" in a high-pitched voice that intermittently intones an interrogative. Then Cortez returns briefly to the fast tempo before concluding the poem by slowly repeating the phrase "they don't want the people."

In contrast to "U.S./Nigerian Relations" and "For the Brave Young Students of Soweto," in "I Am New York City" Cortez emphasizes the surrealistic method that characterizes much of her poetry:

> i am new york city
> here is my brain of hot sauce
> my tobacco teeth my
> mattress of bedbug tongue
> legs apart   hand on chin
> war on the roof   insults
> pointed fingers   pushcarts
> my contraceptives all[.] (*Coagulations* 9)

The first line serves as a riff chorus for the entire poem, which should be read as a praise poem for New York. That is, Cortez's poem, like Sterling Brown's "Kentucky Blues," is an approximation of the blues singer's celebration of a certain place.[20] But in her celebration, Cortez, as is typical of her style, personifies the city. At the same time, she revises traditional male definitions of toughness and rambunctiousness in the big city by describing the urban experience in rebellious feminine terms. Such is her bodaciousness that she takes "hot sauce" and "tobacco teeth" as contraceptives. The persona's unmitigated gall recalls Cortez's "Carolina Kingston," who is an "imbangala woman" who has "plenty macking motherhood / packed in [her] grief house yea" (*Mouth on Paper* 52).

In addition to describing blues-oriented women's refusal to abide by the restrictions of either black men or white America, Cortez achieves a pyrotechnic breakthrough in "I Am New York City." For instance, the third stanza of the poem appears in print:

> I am new york city of blood
> police and fried pies

> i rub my docks red with grenadine
> and jelly madness in a flow of tokay
> my huge skull of pigeons
> my seance of peeping toms
> my plaited ovaries excuse me
> this is my grime my thigh of
> steelspoons and toothpicks
> i imitate no one[.] (9)

The first line of the printed version does not suggest a pause. But in the recorded version, performing with the bassist Richard Davis, Cortez pauses before enunciating the word "blood" by elongating the /e/ sound in "city."[21] In so doing, she maximizes the power of the "blood" image by simulating an unexpected gunshot. Cortez's vocal experiments call attention to her use of tonal semantics. Nielsen has pointed out that the pitch of Cortez's tone descends progressively in her performances.[22] However, Cortez also incarnates blues singers by alternating the pitch of her voice to replicate the antiphony of blues music. After delivering the first two lines in an even-toned pitch, Cortez begins to simulate the call and response. She raises the pitch in the third line of the stanza and lowers it in the next line until the final word, "tokay," which is chanted with a raised pitch. The call and response pattern is repeated until lines seven through nine, wherein Cortez maintains a raised pitch level. In the concluding line, "i imitate no one," she places a slight emphasis on the word "no." This line is not chanted but spoken in a tone of feminine audaciousness that anticipates such women hip-hop artists as MC Lyte and Eve.

Like many Black Arts poets, Cortez has developed vocal techniques to enhance the power of her affective poetics, and her version of blues poetry often incorporates the compressed imagery associated with other poets of the period. For instance, in the passage above, Cortez combines her personification of New York with a menstrual metaphor. Observe the "ovaries" image and the repeated blood images. Beginning with the word "blood" in the first line, the words "grenadine" and "tokay" that end the third and fourth lines, respectively, also suggest bleeding.

At the same time, though, Cortez's blues/surrealist method, which distinguishes her work from most Black Arts poets, allows her to fuse contradictary imagery. Note that the word "police" comes immediately after "blood." Yet the police image is also linked to the "fried pies" image, which suggests not only soul food but also a style of life in which the pursuit of pleasure ignores considerations of jurisprudence. Cortez's menstrual image points to both the excruciating pain of urban life and the people's determination to persevere. The "grenadine" image evokes the unwritten history of colonization of migrants from the Grenadines and suggests simultaneously the physical labor of New York City dock workers and the sweet taste of pomegranate juice. Finally, in the fourth line, the phrase "madness in a flow of" suggests violence and anticipates the word "blood." But like Hughes in "Dream Boogie," Cortez frustrates the reader's expectation with the word "tokay." The term "jelly" is a well-known term of (re)memory that suggests sexual activity. In sandwiching the phrase "madness in a flow" between "jelly" and "tokay," Cortez again describes both the physical dangers of living in New York and its capacity to foster uninhibited fun.

"Lynch Fragment 2" is Cortez's contemporary version of the African American lynch poem. The accompanying music on the recorded version of the poem is not a sorrowful dirge, as one might expect. Instead, Davis introduces the poem with a version of reveille, a bugle call that awakens military personnel in the morning and alerts them for assembly. The irony, of course, is that Davis's performance is itself a wake-up call and summons for action against police brutality. As such, his repetition and inversion constitutes a signifying riff. Similarly, Cortez employs an ironic point of view in her revision of the lynch poem made famous by Jean Toomer and Richard Wright. However, unlike previous poems that focused on how white citizens terrorized blacks in the rural South, Cortez turns her attention to the horrors committed by urban policemen. As in "I Am New York City," Cortez employs a blood image to suggest the violence of the city: "I am bleed mouth nod / from an oath in sorrow" (*Coagulations* 16). Though nodding usually suggests agreement, Cortez uses "nod" ironically to suggest the physical movement of the victim's head and the policemen's zeal to ostensibly obey their sworn "oath[s]" to uphold the law, which many misinterpret as a license to inflict violence.

Unlike "Give Me the Red off the Black of the Bullet," which also addresses police brutality, "Lynch Fragment 2" does not contain a riff chorus, nor are there any explicit references to blackness. Observe these lines from the former poem:

> Give me the black on the red of the bullet
> i want to make a tornado
> to make an earthquake
> to make a fleet of stilts
> for the blackness of Claude Reece Jr.
> the blackness called dangerous weapon
> called resisting an arrest
> called nigger threat[.] (20)

In "Lynch Fragment 2" Cortez uses imagery to describe her persona's physical features and ethnic background before allowing him to give his account
of his experience with police:

> i succulent republic of swamp lips
> push forward my head through
> windshields of violence
> to baptise in a typhoon of night sticks
> Scream on me[.] (16)

The first line refers to the relatively large size of black people's lips.[23] Yet it
also suggests the violence suffered by such victims as Rodney King. Cortez
cleverly reverses the stereotype by celebrating a physical trait associated with
ugliness while simultaneously describing the policeman's distorted worldview that is (mis)informed by the myth of white superiority, which in turn
impels them to view such features as attractive targets for violence. The word
"succulent" suggests both the size of the persona's lips and his awareness of
the policeman's reading of the symbolism of such features.

Lines two through four, like the subsequent one-line stanza, describe the actual beating. Note the "night sticks" image. Such is the intensity of the violence
that Cortez aptly employs a "typhoon" metaphor to describe the rapidity and
force of the licks. Yet again, she creates the illusion that the persona is in control
of the action by using the verb "push." Indeed, the imagery suggests suicide:
"i . . . push forward my head through / windshields." However, Cortez is illustrating the absurdity of police brutality by describing the ludicrousness of the
official accounts that policemen often use to absolve themselves from guilt.

The line "[s]cream on me" also suggests violence. The word "scream" is
a term of (re)memory that recalls a history of pain (and pleasure) in African
American cultural history. Hence, the simulation of its sound among blues
musicians and Haki Madhubuti's call for mobilization in his poem "Don't
Cry, Scream." During the early 1970s, when "Lynch Fragment 2" was published, to scream on someone referred to the act of capping, that is, to vio-
late someone through language.[24]

At the same time, Cortez's blues/surrealist method allows her to testify
to the irrepressible nature of her persona's spirit. On the recording, she enun-
ciates each word in the phrase "scream on me" with emphasis and uses an
impertinent tone that is suggestive of the voices of black inner-city youth.

Having suffered a "typhoon" of terror, the persona performs a ritual:
"i've gasolined my belly against suspects" (16). Then he undergoes a meta-
morphosis and calls out:

Attention all units
i call to the fumes
drawn back against steel
against invisible fuck of a cry
to remove its road block flesh of a flunky
and let that rotting become feast
on sapphire of my adobe fangs. (16)

The first line is both a mockery of the police summons and a call for resistance against injustice. In the recorded version, Cortez replicates the tone of a policewoman. The "road block flesh" image not only suggests the practice of repressive measures like setting roadblocks in predominantly black neighborhoods; it also suggests an inability to think. The term "flunky," which was commonly used in black communities in the 1970s, accentuates the idea by suggesting that the policeman's ethics are based upon his ability to serve as a henchman for the ruling class. But since the persona has metamorphosed into a warlike deity, he is able to use the policeman's weapon against himself. Not only is the "flunky" (policeman) "removed" from the streets; he becomes a "feast." The persona uses "adobe fangs" to tear his "flesh."

The use of profanity, which has been controversial in African American poetry, deserves special commentary here. An early example of profanity used as a poetic device can be found in Sterling Brown's "Slim Greer" in which his persona says, "hot damn."[25] During the Black Arts Movement, poets used profanity in an attempt to reflect the language of the street and to signify to black audiences a sense of rebellion—a disregard for the moral and ethical codes that many blacks perceived to be repressive. In this way, poets attempted to convey a sense of defiant exhilaration that they hoped audiences would attempt to convert into action.[26] In "Lynch Fragment 2," the phrase "invisible fuck of a cry" implies the violation of the victim, his pain, and the public's tendency to ignore such violations.

In the concluding lines, Cortez returns to a riff-like restatement of her persona's identity. Whereas he has introduced himself as "bleed mouth nod," he concludes by saying, "i am zest from bad jaw quiver / of aftermath / Come Celebrate Me" (16). Notable here is the repetition of the mouth image. The term "quiver" evokes the toast "Dolomite," in which the main character, Dolomite, tells his uncle, "I see your lips quiverin', but I don't hear a cocksuckin' word you sayin'." When the uncle responds to the insult by "letting out with a left, as quick as a flash," Dolomite tears his head off because "he was just that damn fast."[27] In her poetic narrative, the victimized uncle becomes a bodacious rebel who continues to "talk trash" during and after a

beating. In the concluding line, Cortez emphasizes the word "me" to reinforce the idea of the persona's irrepressibility.

Davis's elegiac bass playing introduces "Rose Solitude," wherein Cortez
personifies the Duke Ellington muse. Though here, too, there is the brag-
gadocio of the blues persona, she employs less antiphony in her own voice,
using instead a softer, sensual tone to simulate a jazz ballad. Cortez begins
the poem by capturing the ambience of the jazz musician's life offstage:

> I am essence of Rose Solitude
> my cheeks are laced with cognac
> my hips sealed with five satin nails
> i carry dreams of romance of new fools and old flames
> between the musk of fat
> and the side pocket of my mink tongue
> Listen to champagne bubble from this solo[.] (*Coagulations* 36)

As a preeminent blues musician, Ellington was relatively well paid. He was
revered by musicians and audiences alike for his inimitable dress style. He
was called Duke because he wore "turtle skinned shoes" and walked with
"canes / made from dead gazelles" (36). Though Cortez herself is a modest
dresser in her own performances, she recognizes Ellington's dress style as a
vital aspect of his performance. An emphasis on attire is also important in
the black church tradition. As the ethnomusicologist Joyce Jackson points
out in her study of gospel quartets, dress is part of the criteria for a successful performance.[28] Black audiences' adulation for a performer's immaculate
dress seems to reflect a worldview that privileges pageantry and beauty.
Though the logical extreme of such reverence in a capitalist society can imply
a reification of consumerism, one can also argue that black audiences' re-
quirement that their performers be stylishly dressed calls into question the
myth of the starving artist.

Cortez uses her surrealistic method to create a poetic collage filled with
seemingly incongruous word pictures that she near-sings in collaboration
with Davis. In addition, Cortez employs a variation of the riff chorus, though
readers and listeners may not detect it immediately because she shifts her key
words after the first line:

> I tell you from stair steps of these navy blue nights
> these metallic snakes
> these flashing fish skins
> and the melodious cry of Shango
> surrounded by sorrow

by purple velvet tears
by cockhounds limping from crosses[.] (36)

After the first line establishes the rhythm, Cortez begins the next three lines with the word "these" and omits the phrase "I tell you from," opting instead to simulate jazz musicians' method of frustrating their listeners' expectations by implying the phrase. Similarly, Cortez begins the conclusion of the passage with the phrase "surrounded by sorrow" and omits the word "surrounded" in the next two lines (36).

The collage effect also simulates blues music. The blend of brilliant colors with Cortez's silky voice produces an exhilarating effect that is comparable to the soothing feelings that compel foot-tapping motions from audience members at jazz concerts. Moreover, her use of color invokes the presence of blues music. The "navy blue nights" image, like the "purple velvet tears," suggests not only the nighttime settings of the performances but also the blues basis of Ellington's music. The snake and Shango (Nigerian god of thunder) images suggest the saxophones and drums, respectively, while "fish skins" implies the sequined dresses worn by the women patrons.

But in describing Ellington's music and history, the persona reveals herself as a priestess who, by virtue of her ability to permeate corporeal and incorporeal substances, engages in a performance of her own that constitutes, in turn, a form of resistance to traditional definitions of womanhood. Though she is susceptible to stage fright, the persona's bravery is such that she can "walk through the eyes of staring lizards" (37). Cortez's persona delivers her narrative chant in great proximity to the audience, "from [the] stair steps," and is yet able to announce:

I tell you from suspenders from two-timing dog odors
from inca frosted lips
nonchalant legs
i tell you from the howling chant of sister Erzulie
and the exaggerated hearts of a hundred pretty women
they loved him[.] (37)

Note the reference to infidelity; the persona acknowledges the hypocrisy "of two-timing dog odors" (37). She has smelled the stench that has seeped, as it were, into Ellington's "suspenders" (37). Yet she accepts his contradictary behavior as an admittedly foul element of the Ellingtonian constitution. At the same time, she is at once inside the very breath of the Haitian sea goddess Erzulie's chant and the "hearts of a hundred pretty women." Equipped with such powers, she is, from all appearances, omnipotent and can conceive of the unimaginable, such as "a caravan of heads made into ten thousand / flowers" (37). The caravan image is an act of epistrophy that alludes to "Caravan," a tune that many associate with Ellington's music even though he did not compose it, just as jazz aficionados associate "My Favorite Things" with John Coltrane.

In "If the Drum Is a Woman," Cortez engages in an intertextual dialogue with Ellington. Although the poem is epistrophic in its repetition of Ellington's suite entitled *A Drum Is a Woman,* "If the Drum Is a Woman" more specifically revises Ellington's "What Else Can You Do with a Drum," which appears on the album. The first part of the song is a narrative performed by Ellington himself that focuses on Carribee Joe, a lover of nature and animals who finds an elaborate drum in the jungle. When Joe touches the drum, it speaks to him and says, "I am not a drum, I am a *woman.* Know me as Madam Zajj, African chantress."[29] After Joe rejects Madam Zajj's appeal to "make beautiful rhythms together," she angrily flies away to Barbados to find another Joe. Then the trumpet section initiates the calypso rhythms in which the Trinidadian singer Ozzie Bailey sings,

> There was a man who lived in Barbados,
> he saw pretty woman one day,
> he took her home and when she got there she turned into a drum.
> It isn't civilized to beat women
> no matter what they do or they say,
> but will somebody tell me what else can you do with a drum?

Cortez's poem displaces Bailey's male voice and revises Ellington's representation of the black woman as sex object. While Ellington envisioned Madam Zajj (inversion of "jazz") as a representation of the subsumptive qualities of blues music,[30] her capability as an enchantress is based largely on her physical beauty. In contrast, Cortez challenges (male) listeners to question their conceptions of gender roles by assuming the role of the secular priestess:

> If the drum is a woman
> why are you pounding your drum into an insane babble
> why are you pistol whipping your drum at dawn
> why are you shooting through the head of your drum
> and making a drum tragedy of drums
> if the drum is a woman
> don't abuse your drum don't abuse your drum don't abuse your drum[.]
>   (*Coagulations* 57–58)

While many of Cortez's recorded poems are introduced by her band, Cortez opens the poem, and the drummer, who is the only band member present, begins to play in the second line, increasing his volume until he reaches a zenith with the word "babble," thus accentuating Cortez's riff chorus with the word "drum." Conversely, Cortez simulates the drum beat by repeating the phrase "don't abuse your drum."

While "If the Drum Is a Woman" is obviously an indictment of violence against women, the poem is not an idealization of women but rather an appeal to male self-control:

> I know the night is full of displaced persons
> I see skins striped with flames
> I know the ugly disposition of underpaid clerks
> they constantly menstruate through the eyes
> I know the bitterness embedded in flesh
> the itching alone can drive you crazy
> I know that this is America
> and chickens are coming home to roost
> on the MX missile
> But if the drum is a woman
> why are you choking your drum
> why are you raping your drum
> why are you saying disrespectful things
> to your mother drum your sister drum
> your wife drum and your infant daughter drum
> if the drum is a woman
> then understand your drum[.] (57)

In the first five lines, Cortez combines interpolation with a nurturing, sympathetic tone to express her understanding of the oppressive conditions that haunt working-class men. At the end of lines one through three and again in line five, Cortez repeats the word "yes." At the beginning of line seven, she interpolates the word "hey." Note also the epistrophic line "and chickens are coming home to roost," which summons the (re)memory of Malcolm X's banishment from the Black Muslims and his subsequent assassination.

The historical victimization of black men notwithstanding, the passage is actually a study of the process whereby (neo)colonized individuals are often black/brown reflections of the colonizer. The implication is that men must confront their illusions about male superiority as part of the ideological apparatus that undergirds their own class and/or racial marginalization. For Cortez, the most effective means of stimulating such an alteration of consciousness involves developing cooperative strategies of resistance whereby men might achieve true liberation and witness firsthand the benefits of gender equality.

In "In the Morning," Cortez engages in a revision of a different sort. Rather than responding to a specific musician, she draws from the wellspring of African American lore, creating a musico-poetic blues form based upon her idea of the shout. While "shout" recalls the (re)memory of the ring shout,[31] an antebellum religious ceremony in which slaves danced counterclockwise to improvised music with refrains, Cortez's song/poem revises more specifically folk blues tunes and/or black religious hymns performed at revival meetings. Like Sterling Brown's "Memphis Blues," "In the Morning" is informed by an aba structure (text, development, and restatement) that is common in jazz compositions and sermons and can be read as a counterpoint to "U.S./Nigerian Relations." Unlike the latter poem, however, "In the Morning" is not polemical. Instead, the sound of the song/poem informs both form and content. Just as bebop musicians employed phrases like "oolya-koo" to express the pleasure and social ramifications inscribed in the blues impulse, so "In the Morning" describes and conveys the sensations of African American self-discovery through the dance of language in which Cortez reenacts the rocking emotional energy reflected in the syncopation, hand clapping, foot stomping, and suggestive gyrations of the shout-ritual.

In the recorded version of "In the Morning,"[32] the Firespitters introduce the piece with a slow tune that blends a down-home beat with a jazzy, urban sound. Although none of the musicians has a solo, the sound of the guitar is apt because guitarists were the preferred instrumentalists among blues vocalists. The blues sound contributes to the poem's appeal by producing the actual sounds that Cortez celebrates via simulation and replication. Thus, in syncretizing different strands of blues, Cortez and the Firespitters demonstrate the artistic possibilities for cultural hybridity, which in turn becomes a metaphor for her revisionary process as she merges aural and visual discourses, transforming the Western tradition of literature through its subsumption of the blues matrix.

Like the persona of "Rose Solitude," the persona in "In the Morning" is also a performer. The blues, she says, "Masquerad[es] in [her] horn like a river / eclipsed to these infantries of dentures of diving / spears" (*Coagulations* 29). Note the weapon imagery and the conflation of voice/instrument and weapon. Though "In the Morning" is an homage to the blues tradition, Cortez reminds readers that blues music is a form of resistance that expresses an African-derived sensibility:

Disguised in my mouth as a swampland
nailed to my teeth like a rising sun
you come out in the middle of fish-scales
you bleed into gourds wrapped with red ants
you syncopate the air with lungs like screams from yazoo
like X rated tongues
and nickel plated fingers of a raw ghost man
you touch brown nipples into knives
and somewhere stripped like a whirlwind
stripped for the shrine room
you sing to me through the side face of a black rooster[.] (28)

Cortez does not refer specifically to blues music; instead, she uses imagery that suggests (pre)blues culture. In the first four lines of the stanza, she employs images that are equally suggestive of many African cultures as well as the American South: gourd, swamp, sun, and ants. Similarly, the fish image suggests both the fish fries in the South and the diet of Africans who lived in close proximity to large bodies of water. Cortez celebrates the creolized slave culture in which the survival of Africanisms assisted in the development of a uniquely African American sensibility, which in turn helped to foster a milieu wherein blues music could be created.

Like Billie Holiday, Cortez simulates jazz improvisation in the structure of her poem by employing her title phrase as a riff chorus that frames an allusion to blues lyrics: "In the morning in the morning in the morning / all over my door like a rooster / in the morning in the morning in the morning" (28). Cortez's riff chorus functions like a break in jazz. It marks a rhythmic departure from the previous pattern of the poem, and she maximizes the effect by varying the tone of the repeated line. The guitarist Bern Nix complements Cortez's break by soloing afterwards, thereby accentuating the simulation of the jazz break. When Cortez returns to her title phrase for the riff chorus, she simulates the rhythm of blues music by varying the pitch of her voice antiphonally, and she experiments with vowel sounds, elongating the /o/ sound in the repeated phrase "let it blow" to simulate the sounds of horn players. The rhythm continues to build until the poem reaches a crescendo:

In the morning in the morning
when peroxide falls on a bed of broken glass
and the sun rises like a polyester ball of menses
in the morning
gonna firedance in the petro
in the morning

turn loose the blues in the funky jungle
in the morning
I said when you see the morning coming like
a two-headed twister
let it blow let it blow
in the morning in the morning
all swollen up like an ocean in the morning
early in the morning
before the cream dries in the bushes
in the morning
when you hear the rooster cry
cry rooster cry
in the morning in the morning in the morning[.] (30)

The sexual imagery here is obvious. The swelling, dried cream, rooster, and cry all suggest coitus and/or pregnancy. Yet the passage does not concern sexuality so much as it illustrates the profound respect for the cycle of life in the sediment of Afro-vernacular epistemology. The shameless embrace of flesh reflected in the gyrations of black dance and the undulating belly rub associated with blues music represent a celebration of re-creation in the ritual of birth. The music of Cortez's riff chorus underscores this idea, linking the diurnal renewal of nature with spiritual rejuvenation, just as preachers chant "in the morning" to provide hope to their congregations. But whereas preachers typically frame conceptualizations of spirituality within the context of the hereafter, Cortez's riff chorus fosters a new dawn imbued with sociopolitical possibility. The politicized conflation of aural and visual calligraphy reflects Cortez's belief that the raucous energy inscribed in the blues idiom can be channeled into a resistive movement to achieve social change.

If "In the Morning" constitutes the dance of African American language, then "You Know" represents its choreography. Despite the superb crafts-(wo)manship in the former poem, "You Know" is perhaps Cortez's best poem. A counterpart to "In the Morning," "You Know" is self-reflexive and a celebration of the blues idiom. However, "You Know" contrasts with "In the Morning" in several respects. Cortez uses the riff chorus intermittently in "In the Morning" to simulate improvisation. However, in "You Know" the riff chorus, "you know," functions like a walking bass: the steady beat allows for the superimposition of antiphonal lines that simulate a solo. Also, while Cortez creates improvisational effects in "You Know," the poem does not concern music so much as it does blues poetics. That is, it describes and exemplifies Cortez's ability to merge script and sound, thereby incarnating secular priesthood. Just as Bessie Smith and other women blues singers demonstrated their committment to their audiences, so Cortez's dedication "(For the people who speak the you know language)" (*Coagulations* 41) illustrates her political identification with working-class blacks who often repeat the phrase "you know" in conversation.

Cortez's dedication also constitutes an act of signifying (in the traditional sense of that word) on many African Americans whose interpellation is manifested in their vehement disapproval of any linguistic habits that deviate from the dominant culture. In using the phrase "you know" as the rhythmic basis of her poem, Cortez demonstrates the poetic potentiality of African American vernacular English. Thus, "You Know" is a response to Hughes's "Low to High" and "High to Low."

After the band breaks into a bluesy, medium-tempo tune, Cortez opens with,

You know
I sure would like to write a blues
you know
a nice long blues
you know
a good feeling to my writing hand
you know
my hand that can bring two pieces of life
together in your ear
you know
one drop of blues turning a paper clip
into three wings and a bone into a revolt
you know
a blues passing up the stereotype symbols
you know
go into the dark meat of a crocodile
and pinpoint the process
you know
into a solo a hundred times
like the first line of Aretha Franklin[.] (41)

The solo image calls attention to the emphasis upon repetition in African American performance. Hip-hop artists today continue the tradition by repeating sequences of rhymes. The allusion to the singer Aretha Franklin indicates that she is an important artistic model for Cortez. The phrase "the first line of Aretha" suggests Franklin's inimitable style, which is recognized im-

mediately by informed listeners. In addition, Cortez's homage to Franklin recalls the privileged position of the black musician in African American communities, that is, the priestess-like role that Franklin served for black women
during her popularity in the 1960s and 1970s. Like Cortez herself, Franklin was
not, in the strict sense, a blues singer. However, the sound of her voice, her
lyrics, and the style in which she rendered them all produced an effect upon
audiences comparable to that of blues musicians.[33] Franklin's performance
of "Respect" is a case in point. Though Otis Redding had recorded the song
earlier, "Redding's version of 'Respect,'" Sherley Anne Williams argues, "was
never made into the metaphor. Black Man/Black Woman or, just as importantly, Black/White relationships that Aretha Franklin's version became. . . .
Aretha characterized respect as something given with force and great effort
and cost. And when she even went so far as to spell the word 'respect,' *we* knew
that this sister wasn't playing around about getting Respect and keeping it."[34]
The word "we" signifies a community of listeners for whom Franklin articu-
lated a set of values that reinforced her listeners' sense of self.

For Cortez, part of the process of creating a blues poetics involves de-
mythologizing blues music. She cautions against stereotyping blues music as
a complilation of lyrics that run "love love love in the ground" (42) and describes the potential that it holds for an effective resistance poetry, that is, a
hard-hitting poetry "that you could all feel at the same time / on the same
level like a Joe Louis punch" (41). Note, for instance, the paper clip image that,
when infused with "one drop of blues," metamorphoses into "three wings,"
which suggests flight and, hence, liberation. Cortez calls for

> a serious blues
> you know
> a significant blues
> you know
> an unsubmissive blues
> you know
> a just because we exist blues
> you know[.] (42)

Cortez's decision to omit the words "song" or "poem" in lines like "an
unsubmissive blues" (which is a repetition of her own album title) not only
attests to her advocacy of a blues poetics but also suggests a double-edged revision of Black Arts poetry. For instance, "You Know" displays all ten of the
qualities that Carolyn Rodgers lists in her taxonomy of Black Arts poetry. "You
Know" "signif[ies]"; it "teach[es]/rap[s]"; it "run[s] down" and "coatpull[s]";

it engages in "mindblow[ing] (fantasy)"; it is "dealin/swingin"; it expresses "*love*"; it is "two faced (irony)"; it "riff[s]"; it is jazz and "du-wah"; and it concerns "getting us together."[35] Yet the poem is also an implicit critique of the cultural nationalism that impeded the full development of a blues poetics. While "You Know" should be read as a response to Amiri Baraka's request for a exclusively *black* poem in "Black Art,"[36] her foregrounding of the blues tradition in the line "i sure would like to write a blues" is a revision of Baraka's Manichaeism. Similarly, "You Know" retorts to Sonia Sanchez's "liberation / poem" wherein she states unequivocally that blues music "ain't culture."[37]

Cortez's version of blues poetry constitutes a profound challenge to literary conventions and demonstrates the eloquence of prefuture blues poetics. While recent performances by other African American poets such as Sonia Sanchez, Kalamu ya Salaam, Askia Toure, and Amiri Baraka demonstrate the popularity of blues poetry among audiences, Cortez's development of vocal techniques and her ability to work regularly with her own band have allowed her to realize the full potentiality of the incarnation of secular priesthood.

CONCLUSION

AS WE GLIMPSE THE INITIAL SUNBEAMS of the twenty-first century, we can gaze at the past while pondering future trajectories of blues poetics. Before Langston Hughes and Sterling Brown experimented with the blues to expose the contradictions of caste and class, Fenton Johnson in 1919 transformed blues energy into a poetic sledgehammer entitled "Tired," which not only rankled James Weldon Johnson but also anticipated the defiance of the Black Arts Movement by fifty years: "'I am tired of work: I am tired of building up somebody else's civilization.'"[1] Other lesser-known poets who did yeoman work include Helene Johnson and Waring Cuney in the 1920s. Frank Marshall Davis published *Black Man's Verse* (1935) and *I Am the American Negro* (1937) during the Depression years. An outspoken critic of racism and American class relations, Davis anticipated the concerns of many contemporary African American poets. In "Jazz Band," for instance, he writes,

Play that thing, you jazz mad fools!
Boil a skyscraper with a jungle
Dish it to 'em sweet and hot—
Ahhhhhhh[.][2]

The problematic jungle image notwithstanding, Davis's image of a boiling skyscraper suggests the revolutionary potential inscribed within jazz, and his cuisine metaphor anticipates today's hip-hop argot.

In the 1940s and 1950s, Margaret Walker, Gwendolyn Brooks, and Bob Kaufman continued the progression of blues poetics. Walker published *For My People* (1942); Brooks published the epistrophic *A Street in Bronzeville*

(1945); and Bob Kaufman, performing his jazz-inspired poetry before beat audiences in the 1950s, anticipated Larry Neal's call for the destruction of the text.[3] A few years later, in the early 1960s, the Umbra Writers Workshop, which included such poets as Tom Dent, Calvin Hernton, Ishmael Reed, Askia Toure, and David Henderson, prefigured the tones and tensions of the late 1960s and early 1970s, when writers like Henry Dumas and Sarah Webster Fabio began to emerge. Dumas was killed by a New York City police officer in 1968 under dubious circumstances, and Fabio was a primal force in the Black Studies movement and an innovator in poetry.

After the Black Arts Movement, many blues poets came to feel the difficulty if not impossibility of creating good art out of rhetoric and found the didacticism of Black Arts poetics constricting. In their search for alternatives, poets like Sterling D. Plumpp riffed on the blues: "I got the blues of a fallen / teardrop."[4] Many others, however, found that the performance of cultural (re)memory was a more suitable form. Some, like Ntozake Shange, turned to poetic life-writing rendered as drama, creating a three-dimensional revision of the blues in *for colored girls who have considered suicide/when the rainbow is enuf* (1977). Other poets, like Yusef Komunyakaa in *Copacetic* (1984) and Harryette Mullen in *Muse and Drudge* (1995), resorted to epistrophy, infusing their poems with the imagery and rhythmic cadences of black song.

In the 1990s a younger generation of poets appeared, and many of them turned toward popular culture. Some, like Pamela Plummer, emerged during the 1980s but began to publish later. Elizabeth Alexander has earned a reputation in poetry and criticism. Other poets, such as Jessica Care Moore, Tony Medina, Ruth Foreman, Kevin Powell, Suheir Hammad, Carl Redux Rux, Saul Williams, Ras Baraka, and Charlie Braxton have shaped their work, in varying degrees, in relation to hip-hop culture. But insofar as their relationship to hip-hop constitutes a new phase of blues poetics, many younger poets present new challenges for critics because their poetry demands that an understanding of hip-hop culture be incorporated into critical analyses.

Like their predecessors, many of today's young poets are concerned with the politics of representation relative to the role of art in cultural politics. In this book, I have examined the long-standing opposition between blues poets and many academic critics. Yet it is important to understand that my blues trope does not accommodate all black poetry. Such a claim would merely return us to a Manichean vision that replicates the (neo)colonizer in blackface. Many African American poets display little interest in black cultural forms. Therefore, I have focused upon a marginalized segment of African American literature, and I have attempted to initiate a dialogue engaging poets, au-

diences, and critics alike. Future critics of blues poetry will benefit from mul-
tidisciplinary training that combines in-depth analysis of vernacular culture
with a wide range of knowledge that may include philosophy, critical theory,
postcolonial theory, modern poetics, linguistics, anthropology, and/or mu-
sicology. *Afro-Blue* is only a beginning, but it is my hope that future studies
will consider the importance of style and resistance in African American poetry. Since black audiences often treat poets as secular priests who address
the unique concerns of their community, critics should approach style as a
method of waging resistance through art. As Amiri Baraka says, "Form is an
aspect of content. It is an ideological choice."[5]

NOTES

Chapter 1: Trouble in Mind

1. William Dean Howells, qtd. in Marcellus Blount, "The Preacherly Text: African American Poetry and Vernacular Performance," *PMLA* 107.3 (1992): 586. See also William Dean Howells, "Life and Letters," *Harper's Weekly,* 27 June 1896, 630.

2. Blount, "Preacherly Text," 110.

3. Paul Laurence Dunbar, qtd. in James Weldon Johnson, Preface to *The Book of American Negro Poetry* (1922; rpt., New York: Harcourt Brace Jovanovich, 1931), 36.

4. W. E. Burghardt Du Bois, *The Souls of Black Folk: Essays and Sketches* (1903; rpt., Cutchogue, N.Y.: Buccaneer Books, 1976), 16.

5. William Stanley Braithwaite, "A Grave Wrong to the Negro," in *The William Stanley Braithwaite Reader,* ed. Philip Butcher (Ann Arbor: University of Michigan Press, 1972), 2. Subsequent references appear parenthetically in the text.

6. Darwin T. Turner, "Afro-American Literary Critics: An Introduction," in *The Black Aesthetic,* ed. Addison Gayle Jr. (Garden City, N.Y.: Doubleday, 1971), 68.

7. Benjamin Brawley, *The Negro in Literature and Art in the United States* (1929; rpt., New York: AMS Press, 1971), 4. Subsequent references appear parenthetically in the text.

8. James Weldon Johnson, "Preface to the First Edition," in *The Book of American Negro Poetry* (1922; rpt. New York: Harcourt Brace Jovanovich, 1931), 9. Subsequent references appear parenthetically in the text.

9. Countee Cullen, qtd. in I. J. Blue, "A Study of Literary Criticism by Some Negro Writers, 1900–1955" (Ph.D. diss., University of Michigan, 1959), 121–22. For Cullen's extended remarks, see Countee Cullen, "Review of *The Weary Blues,* by Langston Hughes," *Opportunity* 4 (Feb. 1926): 73–74.

10. Countee Cullen, Foreword to *Caroling Dusk: An Anthology of Verse by Negro Poets,* ed. Countee Cullen (1927; rpt., New York: Harper and Row, 1955), x.

11. Ibid., ix.

12. Langston Hughes, "The Negro Artist and the Racial Mountain," in *The Black Aesthetic*, ed. Addison Gayle Jr. (Garden City, N.Y.: Doubleday, 1971), 167. Subsequent references appear parenthetically in the text.

13. For a summary of black critics' reactions to *Fine Clothes to the Jew*, see Arnold Rampersad, *The Life of Langston Hughes*, vol. 1: *1902–1941: I, Too, Sing America* (New York: Oxford University Press, 1986), 140. Rampersad notes that William M. Kelley, Eustace Gay, and J. A. Rogers wrote castigating reviews. Kelley called it "about 100 pages of trash," Rogers said that it made him "positively sick," and Gay said that it "disgusts me."

14. Alain Locke, qtd. in ibid., 145.

15. Alain Locke, "Review of *The Weary Blues*, by Langston Hughes," in *The Critical Temper of Alain Locke: A Selection of His Essays on Art and Culture*, ed. Jeffrey C. Stewart (New York: Garland, 1983), 43.

16. Ibid., 41.

17. Alain Locke, "Propaganda—or Poetry?" in *The Critical Temper of Alain Locke: A Selection of His Essays on Art and Culture*, ed. Jeffrey C. Stewart (New York: Garland, 1983), 43.

18. Ibid., 55.

19. See Fredric Jameson, *The Political Unconscious: Narrative as a Socially Symbolic Act* (Ithaca, N.Y.: Cornell University Press, 1981), 98–99.

20. Alain Locke, "Sterling Brown: The New Negro Poet," in *Voices from the Harlem Renaissance*, ed. Nathan Irvin Huggins (New York: Oxford University Press, 1976), 256.

21. Sterling Brown, *Negro Poetry and Drama* (Washington, D.C.: Associates in Negro Folk Education, 1937), 45. Subsequent references appear parenthetically in the text.

22. Sterling Brown, "The Approach of the Creative Artist to Studies in Folklore," *Journal of American Folklore* 54 (Oct. 1946): 506.

23. Houston Baker, *Blues, Ideology, and Afro-American Literature: A Vernacular Theory* (Chicago: University of Chicago Press, 1984), 68–69.

24. Richard Wright, "Blueprint for Negro Writing," in *The Black Aesthetic*, ed. Addison Gayle Jr. (Garden City, N.Y.: Doubleday, 1971), 320. Subsequent references appear parenthetically in the text.

25. Richard Wright, "The Literature of the Negro in the United States," in *Black Expression: Essays by and about Black Americans in the Creative Arts*, ed. Addison Gayle (New York: Weybright and Talley, 1969), 198–229. Subsequent references appear parenthetically in the text. See also the original version, "Litterature noire americaine," *Les Temps Moderne* 4 (1948): 193–221.

26. John Blassingame, *The Slave Community: Plantation Life in the Antebellum South* (New York: Oxford University Press, 1979), 142.

27. Baker, *Blues, Ideology, and Afro-American Literature*, 71.

28. J. Saunders Redding, *To Make a Poet Black* (1939; rpt., College Park, Md.: McGrath, 1968), 3. Subsequent references appear parenthetically in the text.

29. Margaret Walker, "New Poets," in *Black Expression: Essays by and about Black Americans in the Creative Arts*, ed. Addison Gayle (New York: Weybright and Talley, 1969), 90. Subsequent references appear parenthetically in the text.

30. LeRoi Jones (Amiri Baraka), "The Myth of a Negro Literature," in *Home: Social Essays* (New York: Morrow, 1966), 108. Subsequent references appear parenthetically in the text.

31. See Jennifer Jordan, "Cultural Nationalism in the 1960s: Poetry and Politics,"

in *Race, Politics, and Culture: Critical Essays on the Radicalism of the 1960s*, ed. Adolph Reed (Westport, Conn.: Greenwood Press, 1986), 29–61. Jordan quotes Baraka in a 1969 speech at Rockland Park: "'The Negro artist who is not a nationalist at this late date is a white artist, even without knowing it'" (42). For the full text of Baraka's speech, see "Black Art, Nationalism, Organization, Black Institutions (A Speech Given at Rockland Palace, January 17, 1969)" in *Raise, Race, Rays, Raze* (New York: Random House, 1971), 97–101.

32. Cheryl A. Wall, "Response," in *Afro-American Literary Study in the 1990s*, ed. Houston A. Baker Jr. and Patricia Redmond (Chicago: University of Chicago Press, 1989), 185. Paul Laurence Dunbar, *Lyrics of Love and Laughter* (1903; rpt., New York: Dodd, Mead, 1910), 82.

Chapter 2: Meditations

1. For a compelling critique of cultural nationalism, see Jordan, "Cultural Nationalism in the 1960s." Jordan writes insightfully about the proscriptive nature of cultural nationalism and Black Arts poets' revision of the sermon form. However, like most academics, her analysis of the role of culture in (neo)colonial situations denies the possibility of dialogism and is thereby trapped in the same binary logic that she identifies in Black Arts writing.

2. Ibid., 29.

3. Cecil Taylor, qtd. in Karton Edward Hester, *The Melodic and Polyrhythmic Development of John Coltrane's Spontaneous Composition in a Racist Society* (Lewiston, N.Y.: Edwin Mellen Press, 1997), 65.

4. Hayden White, qtd. in Charles Mills, *The Racial Contract* (Ithaca, N.Y.: Cornell University Press, 1997), 43.

5. Mills, *The Racial Contract*, 43.

6. Extract from the 1798 American edition of *Encyclopaedia Britannica*, qtd. in Emmanuel Chukuudi Eze, ed., *Race and the Enlightenment* (Cambridge, Mass.: Blackwell, 1997), 93–94.

7. Larry Neal, "The Black Arts Movement," in *The Norton Anthology of African American Literature*, ed. Henry Louis Gates Jr. and Nellie Y. McKay (New York: W. W. Norton, 1997), 1960.

8. Lorenzo Thomas, "Ascension: Music and the Black Arts Movement," in *Jazz among the Discourses*, ed. Krin Gabbard (Durham, N.C.: Duke University Press, 1995), 259.

9. Karl Marx, *The German Ideology* (New York: International Publishers, 1947), 64–65.

10. Louis Althusser, "Ideology and Ideological State Apparatuses (Notes towards an Investigation)," in *Lenin and Philosophy and Other Essays* (New York: Monthly Review Press, 1971), 146–47 n.11.

11. Davis has commented on this issue on many occasions. See, for instance, her memoir, *Angela Davis: An Autobiography* (1974; rpt., New York: International Publishers, 1988), 161. See also Elaine Brown's account of the Black Panther party, *A Taste of Power* (New York: Pantheon Books, 1992).

12. Paul D'Amato, "The Communist Party and Black Liberation in the 1930s," *International Socialist Review* 1 (Summer 1997): 35.

13. See Cedric J. Robinson, *Black Marxism* (Atlantic Highlands, N.J.: Zed Books, 1983), 424.

14. Richard Wright, qtd. in ibid., 424.

15. Susan Campbell, "'Black Bolsheviks' and Recognition of African-Americans' Right to Self-Determination by the Communist Party USA," *Science and Society* 58.4 (Winter 1994–95): 448.

16. Ibid.

17. See Rebecca Zurier, *Art for the Masses* (Philadelphia: Temple University Press, 1988), 16.

18. Amiri Baraka, *The Autobiography of LeRoi Jones* (New York: Freundlich Books, 1984), 220. It is important to note, however, that during her incarceration for murder, conspiracy, and kidnapping, Angela Davis received considerable support from the Communist party. See Davis, *Angela Davis.*

19. Amiri Baraka, *Autobiography of LeRoi Jones,* 216.

20. Kalamu ya Salaam, "Black Arts Movement: Spanning the Period from the Mid-1960s to the Mid-1970s," *ChickenBones: A Journal,* <http:www.nathanielturner.com>, Sept. 7, 2002.

21. I'm indebted to Jerry Ward for this idea.

22. David Lionel Smith, "The Black Arts Movement and Its Critics," *American Literary History* 3 (1991): 106.

23. Don L. Lee (Haki Madhubuti), *Dynamite Voices: Black Poets of the 1960s* (Detroit: Broadside, 1971). Subsequent references appear parenthetically in the text.

24. The expletive in question can be read in a dialogic context. On the one hand, the term clearly denotes misogyny; on the other hand, black poets have attempted to use the term to represent a style of life that, though shaped by the dominant superstructure, challenges the ideas within it. See Carolyn Rodgers's poem "The Last M.F.," which addresses the debate about language in the movement, in *Understanding the New Black Poetry: Black Speech and Black Music as Poetic References,* ed. Stephen Henderson (New York: William Morrow, 1973), 346.

25. Conversation with Lorenzo Thomas (Sept. 2000), who, like Henderson, was a member of the Umbra writers group.

26. See Jordan, "Cultural Nationalism in the 1960s," 41.

27. Carolyn Rodgers, "Black Poetry—Where It's At," *Negro Digest* 18–19 (Sept. 1969): 8.

28. See Karla F. C. Holloway, *Moorings and Metaphors: Figures of Culture and Gender in Black Women's Literature* (New Brunswick, N.J.: Rutgers University Press, 1992), 41.

29. Qtd. in Rodgers, "Black Poetry," 10.

30. Zora Neale Hurston, "Characteristics of Negro Expression," in *The Jazz Cadence of American Culture,* ed. Robert G. O'Meally (New York: Columbia University Press, 1998), 298–310.

31. I am borrowing Houston Baker's idea here. See his *Blues, Ideology, and Afro-American Literature.*

32. Rodgers, "Black Poetry," 10.

33. Carolyn M. Rodgers, "Uh Nat'chel Thang—The WHOLE TRUTH—US," *Black World,* Sept. 1971, 5–14. Subsequent references appear parenthetically in the text.

34. Stephen Henderson, *Understanding the New Black Poetry: Black Speech and Black Music as Poetic References* (New York: William Morrow, 1973). Subsequent references appear parenthetically in the text.

35. It is worth noting here that Black Arts theorists' emphasis upon sound was anticipated by Charles Olson in his seminal essay "Projective Verse" (1951), wherein he posits that the fundamental unit of poetry is the poet's breath; which is to say, voice and sound are central, not marginal, to poetry. Transcribing the poem on the page requires skill. See Charles Olson, "Projective Verse," in *Human Universe and Other Essays,* ed. Donald Allen (New York: Grove Press, 1967), 51–61. Critics disagree, though, over the relationship between Olson's theories and Black Arts concepts. For instance, Lorenzo Thomas sees a direct relationship between Olson and the Black Arts writers. He points out that Amiri Baraka cites Olson's essay as exemplary in his 1960 essay "How You Sound." Stephen Henderson, however, has expressed skepticism toward the idea that Black Arts poets were directly influenced by Olson. Henderson notes that while Baraka was certainly central to the movement, he was not a metonym. Many poets came from different backgrounds and therefore employed different strategies in their work. Furthermore, Baraka has acknowledged that both Larry Neal and Askia Toure were models of his nationalist poetry. My own hypothesis is that similar ideas were floating around the country in various places and spaces in time. Perhaps jazz musicians' improvisational theories became infused into the larger fabric of the culture? Observe, for instance, Langston Hughes's longstanding experiments with sound; and his *Montage of a Dream Deferred* (which he recorded with the bassist Charles Mingus) appeared during the same year as Olson's "Projective Verse." Lurking beneath the surface of this disagreement, I think, is the issue of cultural authority. Aldon Lynn Nielsen has discussed white critics' reluctance to acknowledge black antecedents to white avant-garde literature. See his *Black Chant: Languages of African-American Postmodernism* (New York: Cambridge University Press, 1997), 71.

My point here is that Anglo-American critics have traditionally expressed skepticism that African American culture might spawn ideas that could lead to an avantgarde literary discourse. This is clearly Henderson's thinking when he says that Black Arts poets believed that "excellence of craft and relevance of statement depended on a deep involvement in the culture and the lives of the people. This assumption, unfortunately, was not always considered by critics who had their own notions of poetry and how best to judge it. . . . One such [notion] is Charles Olson's theory of 'projective verse.'" See Henderson, "Worrying the Line: Notes on Black American Poetry," in *The Line in Postmodern Poetry,* ed. Robert Frank and Henry Sayre (Urbana: University of Illinois Press, 1988), 61–62. Yet in relation to the critical writing, the question of direct influence is moot; the more fundamental question concerns the nature of the critical project at hand. Since the present project focuses specifically upon African American cultural history and critical responses to it, I have chosen not to examine the parallels between Olson's work and Black Arts theorists. For a thorough investigation of the linkages between Black Mountain poetics and black poetry, see Nathaniel Mackey, *Discrepant Engagement: Dissonance, Cross-Culturality, and Experimental Writing* (New York: Cambridge University Press, 1993). See also Lorenzo Thomas, *Extraordinary Measures: Afrocentric Modernism and Twentieth-Century American Poetry* (Tuscaloosa: University of Alabama Press, 2000).

36. See Houston Baker's analysis of the controversy in *Blues, Ideology, and Afro-American Literature,* 64–112.

37. Destiny's Child, "Bootylicious," *Survivor* (Columbia 07464610632).

38. Big Tymers, "Get Your Roll On," *I Got That Work* (Universal 4228609972).

39. Larry Neal, *Visions of a Liberated Future: Black Arts Movement Writings,* ed. Michael Schwarz (New York: Thunder's Mouth, 1989), 46. Subsequent references appear parenthetically in the text.

40. Smith, "The Black Arts Movement and Its Critics," 106.

41. I am borrowing Jerry Ward's idea here. See Jerry W. Ward Jr., Introduction to *Trouble the Water: 250 Years of Afro-American Poetry,* ed. Jerry W. Ward Jr. (New York: Penguin Group, 1997), xx.

42. See Jordan, "Cultural Nationalism in the 1960s," 31–32. Jordan sees Neal as a "decidedly apolitical" (31) critic who merely wants to "conserve the tradition" (32), yet Neal's keen knowledge of the blues qua blues and its relationship to such cultural figures as Malcolm X, John Coltrane, and James Brown illustrates his understanding of the African American culture and politics as infinitely dynamic and, finally, perfectly capable of providing the germs for alternate conceptualizations of base and superstructure.

43. See Frantz Fanon, *The Wretched of the Earth,* trans. Constance Farrington (1968; rpt., New York: Grove Press, 1979), 148–57.

44. Askia Toure, personal interview with the author, 21 Sept. 1995. See also Tony Bolden, "Art and Struggle: An Interview with Amiri Baraka," in *The Ark of the Spirit,* ed. Quo Vadis Gex-Breaux (Atlanta: National Black Arts Festival, 1996), 33.

45. Edward Kamau Brathwaite, *History of the Voice: The Development of Nation Language in Anglophone Caribbean Poetry* (London: New Beacon Books, 1984), 30.

46. Henry Louis Gates Jr., *Figures in Black: Words, Signs, and the Racial Self* (New York: Oxford University Press, 1987), 32.

47. Barbara Harlow, *Resistance Literature* (New York: Methuen, 1987), 50.

48. D. H. Melhem, *Heroism in the New Black Poetry: Introductions and Interviews* (Lexington: University Press of Kentucky, 1990), 4–6.

49. Sonia Sanchez, *We a BaddDDD People* (Detroit: Broadside Press, 1970), 36.

50. This phrase, which meant black on the outside and white on the inside, referred to blacks who identified politically with the dominant culture. Toni Morrison, in her novel *The Bluest Eye,* revises the phrase in relation to her character, Maureen Peal, a light-skinned African American girl who attacks Claudia, her sister Frieda, and their friend, Pecola, by calling them "Black and ugly black e mos," while proclaiming that she is "cute." In response, Claudia and Frieda call Maureen "Meringue Pie." Maureen's complexion, traditionally referred to as yellow in black vernacular, along with the lemon-pie image (peal and meringue), suggests that she is yellow on the outside and white in the inside, that is, an interpellated subject. See Toni Morrison, *The Bluest Eye* (1970; rpt., New York: Alfred A. Knopf, 2000), 73.

51. Malcolm X, qtd. in Amiri Baraka, "Malcolm X as Ideology," in *Malcolm X: In Our Own Image,* ed. Joe Wood (New York: St. Martin's Press, 1992), 31.

52. See Fanon, *The Wretched of the Earth.*

53. Irish Catholics, besieged by violent opposition to Catholic children attending school in Northern Ireland, have likened their experience to the 1963 bombing in Birmingham during which four black girls were killed.

54. Lorenzo Thomas, qtd. in Charles H. Rowell, "Between the Comedy of Matters and the Ritual Workings of Man," *Callaloo* 4 (1981): 24.

55. Melhem, *Heroism in the New Black Poetry,* 6.

Chapter 3: Elaborations

1. Harlow, *Resistance Literature,* 60.

2. Ibid., 37.

3. Patrick Taylor, *The Narrative of Liberation: Perspectives on Afro-Caribbean Literature, Popular Culture, and Politics* (Ithaca, N.Y.: Cornell University Press, 1989), 80.

4. Albert Murray, *Stomping the Blues* (1976; rpt., New York: Da Capo Press, 1987), 45. Subsequent references appear parenthetically in the text.

5. Abbey Lincoln, *Straight Ahead* (Candid ccd 79015a).

6. Lawrence W. Levine, *Black Culture and Black Consciousness: Afro-American Folk Thought from Slavery to Freedom* (New York: Oxford University Press, 1977), 239–40. Subsequent references appear parenthetically in the text.

7. Steven C. Tracy, *Langston Hughes and the Blues* (Urbana: University of Illinois Press, 1988), 59. Subsequent references appear parenthetically in the text.

8. Robert Palmer, *Deep Blues* (New York: Penguin Books, 1981), 25.

9. Ben Sidran, *Black Talk* (New York: Holt, Rinehart and Winston, 1971), 21.

10. William Barlow, *"Looking Up at Down": The Emergence of Blues Culture* (Philadelphia: Temple University Press, 1989), 23–24. Subsequent references appear parenthetically in the text.

11. Jon Michael Spenser, *Blues and Evil* (Knoxville: University of Tennessee Press, 1993), 44.

12. Ibid., 44–45.

13. Sippie Wallace, "Section Hand Blues" (Okeh 8232).

14. See Bolden, "Art and Struggle," 32.

15. Dude Botley, qtd. in Neal, *Visions of a Liberated Future,* 108–9.

16. Eric Hobsbaum, qtd. in Paul Garon, *Blues and the Poetic Spirit* (1975; rpt., New York: De Capo Press, 1978), 53.

17. Ralph Ellison, "Richard Wright's Blues," in *The Collected Essays of Ralph Ellison,* ed. John F. Callahan (New York: Modern Library, 1995), 129.

18. Reverend Rubin Lacy, qtd. in Jeff Todd Titon, *Early Downhome Blues: A Musical and Cultural Analysis* (Urbana: University of Illinois Press, 1977), 43.

19. Baker, *Blues, Ideology, and Afro-American Literature,* 5.

20. Ibid., 3.

21. Robert Farris Thompson, *Flash of the Spirit: African and Afro-American Art and Philosophy* (New York: Vintage Books, 1983), xiii.

22. Palmer, *Deep Blues,* 66.

23. Qtd. in ibid., 42.

24. Dee Dee Bridgewater, *Love and Peace* (Verve Records 314 527 470-2); The Roots, *The Roots Come Alive* (MCA 0881120592).

25. Eric Dolphy, qtd. in Nat Hentoff's liner notes for Eric Dolphy, *Far Cry* (Fantasy OJC-400, NJ-8270).

26. Stuart Hall, "What Is This 'Black' in Black Popular Culture?" in *Black Popular Culture,* ed. Gina Dent (1983; rpt., New York: New Press, 1998), 27.

27. It is worth noting that there was indeed writing in traditional African cultures. See Thompson, *Flash of the Spirit,* 244–48.

28. Sidran, *Black Talk,* 9.

29. Nielsen, *Black Chant*, 3–37.

30. Richard Bauman, *Verbal Art as Performance* (1977; rpt., Prospect Heights, Ill.: Waveland Press, 1984), 9.

31. Jeff Todd Titon, "Thematic Pattern in Downhome Blues Lyrics: The Evidence on Commercial Phonograph Records since World War II," *Journal of American Folklore* 87 (1974): 318.

32. John Coltrane, qtd. in Frank Kofsky, *Black Nationalism and the Revolution in Music* (1970; rpt., New York: Pathfinder Press, 1991), 225.

33. Qtd. in James Cone, *The Spirituals and the Blues: An Interpretation* (New York: Seabury Press, 1972), 23.

34. Qtd. in Vincent Harding, *There Is a River: The Black Struggle for Freedom in America* (New York: Random House, 1981), 103.

35. Angela Davis, *Blues Legacies and Black Feminism* (New York: Vintage, 1998), 113.

36. Sidney Finkelstein, *How Music Expresses Ideas* (1952; rpt., New York: International Publishers, 1976), 10–11.

37. Samuel Charters, qtd. in Baker, *Blues, Ideology, and Afro-American Literature*, 188. See also Cone, *The Spirituals and the Blues*, 109.

38. Cone, *The Spirituals and the Blues*, 114.

39. Ibid., 112.

40. Sidran, *Black Talk*, 19.

41. Gene Gilmore, "The Natchez Fire," qtd. in John Michael Spenser, *Blues and Evil* (Knoxville: University of Tennessee Press, 1993), 48

42. Dizzie Gillespie with Al Fraser, *To BE, or Not . . . to BOP* (Garden City, N.Y.: Doubleday, 1979), 488. Subsequent references appear parenthetically in the text.

43. John Coltrane, liner notes, *A Love Supreme* (Impulse A-77).

44. Albert Murray, *The Omni-Americans: New Perspectives on Black Experience and American Culture* (New York: Outerbridge and Dienstrfrey, 1970), 147.

45. Miles Davis with Quincy Troupe, *Miles: The Autobiography* (New York: Simon and Schuster, 1989), 361 (my italics).

46. Titon, "Thematic Patterns in Downhome Blues Lyrics," 318.

47. Chris Albertson, qtd. in Davis, *Blues Legacies and Black Feminism*, 96.

48. Locke, "Propaganda—Or Poetry?" 55.

49. Bessie Smith, "Poor Man's Blues" (Columbia 14399-D). See Daphne Duval Harrison, *Black Pearls: Blues Queens of the 1920s* (New Brunswick, N.J.: Rutgers University Press, 1988), 71.

50. See Fanon, *The Wretched of the Earth*, 148–205.

51. Untitled folk blues lyric, qtd. in Langston Hughes and Arna Bontemps, *The Book of Negro Folklore* (New York: Dodd, Mead, 1958), 384.

52. Qtd. in Paul Oliver, *Blues Fell This Morning: Meaning in the Blues* (1960; rpt., New York: Cambridge University Press, 1990), 15.

53. Untitled folk blues lyric, qtd. in Cone, *The Spirituals and the Blues*, 139.

54. Titon, "Thematic Patterns in Downhome Blues Lyrics," 323.

55. Texas Alexander, *Alger "Texas" Alexander: Texas Troublesome Blues* (Agram Blues AB 2009).

56. Peetie Wheatstraw, "The Good Lawd's Children" (Decca 7879).

57. Big Bill Broonzy, "Looking Up at Down" (Okeh 05698).

58. Untitled folk blues lyric, qtd. in Hughes and Bontemps, *The Book of Negro Folklore,* 395.

59. Victoria Spivey, "Bloodhound Blues" (Okeh 8339).

60. Eve, "Love Is Blind," *Let There Be . . . Eve—Ruff Ryders' First Lady* (Ruff Ryders/Interscope 0694904532).

61. TLC, "No Scrubs," *Fanmail* (LaFace/Arista AC 26055–4).

62. Lizzie Miles, "I Hate a Man Like You" (RCA Victor LPV 508).

63. Harrison, *Black Pearls,* 89.

64. Sara Evans, qtd. in Davis, *Blues Legacies and Black Feminism,* 25.

65. Gertrude "Ma" Rainey, "Prove It on Me Blues" (Paramount 12668). Reissued on *Ma Rainey* (Milestone M-47021).

66. Davis, *Blues Legacies and Black Feminism,* xii.

67. Afro-vernacular phrase popularized by the rapper Master P. The phrase "bout-it, bout-it" denotes firm determination regardless of the circumstances.

68. Mahalia Jackson, "How I Got Over," *In My Heart* (New Media B00005TSP2).

69. The Dirty Dozen Brass Band, "Blue Monk/Stormy Monday," *The Dirty Dozen Brass Band Live: Mardi Gras in Montreux* (Rounder Records 2052).

70. Kalamu ya Salaam, liner notes, *The Dirty Dozen Brass Band Live.*

71. See Kofsky, *Black Nationalism and the Revolution in Music,* 279–80. Kofsky states that Handy's "If We Only Knew" (Columbia CL 2462) bears a striking resemblance to Coltrane's "Spiritual" (Pablo Live 2620 101).

72. See LeRoi Jones (Amiri Baraka), *Blues People: The Negro Experience in White America and the Music That Developed from It* (New York: William Morrow, 1963), 196.

73. Margaret Walker, "Kissie Lee," in *Black Sister: Poetry by Black American Women, 1746–1980,* ed. Erlene Stetson (Bloomington: Indiana University Press, 1981), 95.

74. Arthur "ARTURO" Pfister, "Stagolee and Billy," in *From a Bend in the River,* ed. Kalamu ya Salaam (New Orleans: Runagate Press, 1998), 167–72. All subsequent references appear parenthetically in the text.

75. Stagolee is often referred to as Stackolee.

76. See Henderson, *Understanding the New Black Poetry,* 330–31.

77. Traditional version popular in the San Francisco–Oakland Bay Area.

78. Shirley Williams, "Say Hello to John," in *The Peacock Poems* (Middletown, Conn.: Wesleyan University Press, 1975), 14.

79. Geneva Smitherman, *Talkin and Testifyin: The Language of Black America* (1977; rpt., Detroit: Wayne State University Press, 1985), 26. Subsequent references appear parenthetically in the text.

80. Thelonius Monk, "Epistrophy," *Thelonius Monk with John Coltrane* (Riverside OJCCD-039-2).

81. Sterling Stuckey, *Slave Culture: Nationalist Theory and the Foundations of Black America* (New York: Oxford University Press, 1987), 96.

82. Wynton Marsalis, qtd. in Stanley Crouch's liner notes, "The Majesty of the Blues," on Marsalis's *The Majesty of the Blues* (Columbia 45091).

83. Sidran, *Black Talk,* 67.

84. Henderson, *Understanding the New Black Poetry,* 44.

85. Henry Louis Gates Jr., *The Signifying Monkey: A Theory of Afro-American Literary Criticism* (New York: Oxford University Press, 1988), 123 (my italics).

86. Alvin Aubert, "Black American Poetry, Language, and the Folk Tradition," *Black Academy Review* 2 (1971): 74.

87. Robert Hayden, "Runagate Runagate," in *The Poetry of Black America,* ed. Arnold Adoff (New York: Harper and Row, 1973), 120–22. Subsequent references appear parenthetically in the text.

88. Alvin Aubert, *South Louisiana: New and Selected Poems* (Grosse Point Farms, Mich.: Lunchroom Press, 1985), 63.

89. Alvin Aubert, personal letter to the author, 17 Mar. 2000. I am indebted to Mr. Aubert for providing the inspiration for the following discussion.

90. See Stuckey, *Slave Culture,* 19. Particularly cogent here is Stuckey's observation of how bebop is prefigured in representations of black musicians in antebellum folktales.

91. Larry Neal, "The Life: Hoodoo Hollerin' Bebop Ghosts," in *Hoodoo Hollerin' Bebop Ghosts* (Washington, D.C.: Howard University Press, 1974), 3.

92. I might add here that freestyling itself precedes hip-hop. As a member of my high school track team, I witnessed and participated in such performances regularly. After our meets, which we invariably won, the coach allowed us to celebrate by performing our "Theme Song," which consisted of a rhythm established by clapping in unison, while performers stood up and created rhymes that poked fun at various members' performances during their events. Nobody was spared, not even people who set records in their events. Yet tempers never flared because it was understood that the comments were made in the spirit of fun.

93. Amiri Baraka, "Speech #38 (Or Y We Say It This Way)," in *Transbluesency: The Selected Poems of Amiri Baraka/LeRoi Jones, 1961–1995,* ed. Paul Vangelisti (New York: Marsilio, 1995), 258–62. Subsequent references appear parenthetically in the text.

94. Miles Davis, *The Complete Birth of the Cool* (Capitol Jazz CDP72439455023).

95. Langston Hughes, "Ballad of the Landlord," in *The Collected Poems of Langston Hughes,* ed. Arnold Rampersad (New York: Alfred A. Knopf, 1995), 402–3.

96. There are many accounts of this story. It seems that Monk was in a car with the pianist Bud Powell when two police officers approached the car. Drugs were found, and although there was never any proof that Monk was using the drug or involved in a transaction, he was convicted of possession, which made it impossible to obtain a cabaret card because the New York City Police Department, which required anyone working in clubs to have one, refused to issue such a card to anyone who had been convicted of such a crime. It is a testimony to Monk's commitment to his art that he continued to compose nonetheless. See Leslie Gourse, *Straight, No Chaser: The Life and Genius of Thelonius Monk* (New York: Schimer Books, 1997).

97. I am borrowing Aldon Lynn Nielsen's idea here. See Nielsen, *Black Chant.*

98. Raymond Williams, *Marxism and Form* (New York: Oxford University Press, 1977), 47.

99. Quo Vadis Gex-Breaux, telephone interview with the author, 6 Dec. 1995.

100. Melhem, *Heroism in the New Black Poetry,* 5.

101. Ibid., 3.

102. Here I am not referring simply to rap as a component of hip-hop but to the entire tradition of black rappers.

103. Bauman, *Verbal Art as Performance,* 19.

104. Finkelstein, *How Music Expresses Ideas,* 10–11.

105. I owe this idea to Jerry W. Ward Jr.

106. Stuckey, *Slave Culture,* 66.

107. Mezz Mezzrow, qtd. in Gates, *The Signifying Monkey,* 70 (my italics).

108. Davis with Troupe, *Miles,* 375.

109. Haki Madhubuti, "But He Was Cool," in *Don't Cry, Scream* (1969; rpt., Chicago: Third World Press, 1992), 24–25. Subsequent references appear parenthetically in the text.

110. Thompson, *Flash of the Spirit,* 16.

111. Quo Vadis Gex-Breaux, "Jazz Rain," *New Laurel Review* 17 (1990): 22. Subsequent references appear parenthetically in the text.

112. Quo Vadis Gex-Breaux, telephone interview with the author, 6 Dec. 1995.

113. Ibid.

114. Kalamu ya Salaam, "Art for Life: My Story, My Song," *Contemporary Authors Series* 21 (1995): 193.

115. Kalamu ya Salaam with Percussion Incorporated, "Congo Square," *My Story, My Song* (AFO Records 95-1128-2).

116. Robert Farris Thompson, "Kongo Influences on African-American Artistic Culture," in *Africanisms in American Culture,* ed. Joseph E. Holloway (Bloomington: Indiana University Press, 1990), 150.

117. Gerald L. Davis, *I Got the Word in Me and I Can Sing It, You Know: A Study of the Performed African-American Sermon* (Philadelphia: University of Pennsylvania Press, 1985), 30.

118. Ibid., 33.

119. Salaam, "Art for Life," 224.

120. Houston Baker, "Critical Change and Blues Continuity," in *Afro-American Poetics: Revisions of Harlem and the Black Aesthetic* (Madison: University of Wisconsin Press, 1988), 158.

121. Thompson, *Flash of the Spirit,* 9. See also Robert L. Hall, "African Religious Retentions in Florida," in *Africanisms in American Culture,* ed. Joseph E. Holloway (Bloomington: Indiana University Press, 1990), 111.

Chapter 4: Early Blues Poetics

1. Murray, *Stomping the Blues,* 211.

2. Rollin Harte, qtd. in Redding, *To Make a Poet Black,* 98.

3. W. E. B. Du Bois, qtd. in David Levering Lewis, *When Harlem Was in Vogue* (New York: Random House, 1981), 15. Subsequent references appear parenthetically in the text.

4. Oliver, *Blues Fell This Morning,* 282.

5. Johnson, Preface to *The Book of American Negro Poetry,* 4.

6. Joanne Gabbin, *Sterling A. Brown: Building the Black Aesthetic Tradition* (Westport, Conn.: Greewood Press, 1985), 5. Subsequent references appear parenthetically in the text.

7. Sterling Brown, qtd. in Eugene B. Redmond, *Drumvoices: The Mission of Afro-American Poetry* (Garden City, N.Y.: Anchor Press, 1976), 227–28.

8. Lorenzo Thomas, "Authenticity and Elevation: Sterling Brown's Theory of the Blues," *African American Review* 31 (1997): 412.

9. Sterling Brown, "Negro Characters as Seen by White Authors," *Callaloo* 5 (Feb.–May 1982): 66.

10. Robert G. O'Meally, "Game to the Heart: Sterling Brown and the Badman," *Callaloo* 5 (Feb.–May 1982): 45.

11. Sterling A. Brown, *The Collected Poems of Sterling A. Brown,* ed. Michael S. Harper (New York: Harper and Row, 1980), 20. Subsequent references appear parenthetically in the text.

12. Mark Sanders, *Afro-Modernist Aesthetics and the Poetry of Sterling A. Brown* (Athens: University of Georgia Press, 1999), 9–10.

13. Dudley Randall, *The Black Poets* (New York: Bantam, 1971), 12.

14. Ibid., 13.

15. James Smethurst, *The Red New Negro* (New York: Oxford University Press, 1999), 66.

16. Davis, *Blues Legacies and Black Feminism,* 139.

17. Bessie Smith, "Mama's Got the Blues" (Columbia 14023-D), reissued on *Empty Bed Blues* (Columbia CG30450).

18. Tupac Shakur, "I Get Around," *Strictly 4 My N.I.G.G.A.Z.* (Jive 41634).

19. Brown, "Negro Characters as Seen by White Authors," 73.

20. Zora Neale Hurston, *Their Eyes Were Watching God* (1937; rpt., Urbana: University of Illinois Press, 1978), 29.

21. Qtd. in Barlow, *"Looking Up at Down,"* 52.

22. Oliver, *Blues Fell This Morning,* 192–96.

23. Jones, *Blues People,* 67.

24. Sterling Brown, "Negro Folk Expression: Spirituals, Seculars, Ballads, and Work Songs," *Phylon* 14 (1953): 57.

25. Ibid.

26. Zora Neale Hurston, *Mules and Men* (1935; rpt., Bloomington: Indiana University Press, 1978), 154.

27. Mark A. Sanders, "Distilled Metaphysics: The Dynamics of Voice and Vision in the Poetry of Sterling A. Brown" (Ph.D. diss., Brown University, 1992).

28. Jean Wagner, *Black Poets of the United States: From Paul Laurence Dunbar to Langston Hughes,* trans. Kenneth Douglas (Urbana: University of Illinois Press, 1973), 490.

29. Brown, "Negro Folk Expression," 57.

30. Titon, *Early Downhome Blues,* 29.

31. Nathan Huggins, *Harlem Renaissance* (New York: Oxford University Press, 1971), 226–27.

32. Sterling Stuckey, Introduction to *The Collected Poems of Sterling A. Brown,* ed. Michael S. Harper (New York: Harper and Row, 1980), 11.

33. See Stephen Henderson, "The Heavy Blues of Sterling Brown: A Study of Craft and Tradition," *Black American Literature Forum* 14 (Spring 1980): 37.

34. Henry Thomas, *Henry Thomas: Ragtime Texas* (Herwin 209). See Barlow, *"Looking Up at Down,"* 356 n.2.

35. Hurston, "Characteristics of Negro Expression," 300.

36. Qtd. in Oliver, *Blues Fell This Morning,* 282.

37. Hurston, *Their Eyes Were Watching God*, 16.

38. Titon, *Early Downhome Blues*, 21.

39. Paul Oliver, *Blues Off the Record* (New York: Hippocrene Books, 1984), 19.

40. See Paul Oliver, qtd. in Henderson, "The Heavy Blues of Sterling Brown," 36. I should also point out that Bessie Smith's sister-in-law, Maud Smith, has said that, contrary to most critics' previous claims, "Backwater Blues" was not about the great flood. Rather, Smith got the idea for the song after being asked by a fan whose town was flooded to sing "Backwater Blues," which was not in her repertoire. After returning home, she proceeded to write the song, and its release coincided with the great flood. See Davis, *Blues Legacies and Black Feminism*, 108.

41. Oliver, *Blues Fell This Morning*, 278.

42. Harry Oster, qtd. in Bill Evans, *Big Road Blues: Tradition and Creativity in the Folk Blues* (Berkeley: University of California Press, 1982), 23.

43. Oliver, *Blues Off the Record*, 19.

44. Charles H. Rowell, "Sterling A. Brown and the Afro-American Folk Tradition," in *The Harlem Renaissance Re-examined*, ed. Victor A. Kramer (New York: AMS Press, 1987), 327.

45. Henderson, "The Heavy Blues of Sterling Brown," 40.

46. Ibid., 41.

47. For an insightful discussion of Broonzy's song, see ibid.

48. John O. Killens, qtd. in ibid.

49. Ralph Ellison, *Invisible Man* (1952; rpt., New York: Vintage Books, 1972), chap. 2.

50. Wagner, *Black Poets of the United States*, 490.

51. It is interesting to note that the Atlanta semipro baseball team adopted the Crackers as its monicker.

52. Tony Bolden, "Old Man Joe," in *Word Up: Black Poetry of the 80s From the Deep South* (Atlanta: Beans and Brown Rice Publishers, 1990), 21.

53. Sanders, *Afro-Modernist Aesthetics and the Poetry of Sterling Brown*, 18.

54. Ibid., 21.

Chapter 5: Epistrophy

1. Eric Lott, "Double V, Double-Time: Bebop's Politics of Style," in *Jazz among the Discourses*, ed. Krin Gabbard (Durham, N.C.: Duke University Press, 1995), 245–46.

2. Kenny Clarke, qtd. in Gillespie with Fraser, *To BE or Not . . . to BOP*, 142.

3. Lott, "Double V, Double-Time," 248.

4. Eric Porter, "Out of the Blue: Black Creative Musicians and the Challenge of Jazz, 1940–1995" (Ph.D diss., University of Michigan, 1997), 66. See also Eric Porter, *What Is This Thing Called Jazz?* (Berkeley: University of California Press, 2002), 83–84. For a more extensive discussion, see Bernard Gindron, "A Short Stay in the Sun: The Reception of Bebop (1944–1950)," *Library Chronicle of the University of Texas* 24 (1994): 137–60.

5. Langston Hughes, qtd. in Sascha Feinstein, *Jazz Poetry: From the 1920s to the Present* (Westport, Conn.: Greenwood Press, 1994), 107.

6. Lionel Hampton, qtd. in Lott, "Double V, Double-Time," 51.

7. Langston Hughes, qtd. in Feinstein, *Jazz Poetry*, 108 (my italics).

8. Langston Hughes, *The Collected Poems of Langston Hughes,* ed. Arnold Rampersad and David Roessel (New York: Alfred A. Knopf, 1995), 387. Subsequent references appear parenthetically in the text.

9. I am borrowing W. E. B. Du Bois's title here.

10. See Arnold Rampersad, *The Life of Langston Hughes,* vol. 2: *1941–1967: I Dream of a World* (New York: Oxford University Press, 1988), 153.

11. Ezra Pound, qtd. in Craig Hansen Werner, *Playing the Changes: From Afro-Modernism to the Jazz Impulse* (Urbana: University of Illinois Press, 1994), 165.

12. Ibid., 163.

13. I am borrowing Aldon Lynn Nielsen's idea here. See *Black Chant,* 3–37.

14. In 1958, Hughes and Charles Mingus collaborated on an album that featured *Montage of a Dream Deferred.* See Langston Hughes, Charles Mingus, and Leonard Feather, *Weary Blues* (Verve 841 660-2).

15. See Wagner, *Black Poets of the United States,* 414. See also Michael DeJongh, *Vicious Modernism: Black Harlem and the Literary Imagination* (New York: Cambridge University Press, 1990), 104.

16. I am borrowing Craig Werner's term here.

17. See A. B. Spellman, *Four Lives in the Bebop Business* (New York: Pantheon Books, 1966), 200–201.

18. Art Lange, qtd. in Sascha Feinstein, "Epistrophies: Poems Celebrating Thelonius Monk and His Music," *African American Review* 31 (1996): 57.

19. See Gillespie with Fraser, *To BE, or Not . . . to BOP,* 118–35.

20. Carl Woideck, *Charlie Parker: His Music and Life* (Ann Arbor: University of Michigan Press, 1996), 23.

21. Dickie Wells, qtd. in Gillespie with Fraser, *To BE, or Not . . . to BOP,* 67.

22. Walter C. Farrell Jr. and Patricia A. Johnson, "Poetic Interpretations of Urban Black Folk Culture: Langston Hughes and the "Bebop" Era," *MELUS* 8 (1981): 59. See also Hughes's "Down Under Harlem," *Negro Digest* 11 (Apr. 1944): 7–8. Hughes responds to the reactionary idea that opposition itself is counterproductive.

23. I am borrowing Ralph Ellison's phrase here.

24. See Michere Githae Mugo, *Orature and Human Rights* (Rome: Institute of South African Development Studies, NUL, Lesotho, 1991). See also Davis, *Blues Legacies and Black Feminism,* 25.

25. Tracy, *Langston Hughes and the Blues,* 226.

26. Jones, *Blues People,* 120.

27. Traditional blues verse, qtd. in Murray, *Stomping the Blues,* 62.

28. Jones, *Blues People,* 114–16.

29. Tracy, *Langston Hughes and the Blues,* 234.

30. Jerry W. Ward Jr., Introduction to *Trouble the Water: 250 Years of African-American Poetry,* ed. Jerry W. Ward Jr. (New York: Mentor, 1997), xx.

31. See Leonard Feather, liner notes to Langston Hughes, Charles Mingus, and Leonard Feather, *Weary Blues* (Verve 841 660-2).

Chapter 6: Taking the Blues Back Home

1. Haki Madhubuti, "a poem to complement other poems" in *Don't Cry, Scream,* 36–38. André Breton, "Second Manifesto of Surrealism," in *Manifestoes of Surreal-*

ism, trans. Richard Seaver and Helen R. Lane (Ann Arbor: University of Michigan Press, 1969), 132.

2. Aime Cesaire, *Discourse on Colonialism,* trans. Joan Pinkham (1955; rpt., New York: Monthly Review Press, 1972), 68.

3. Nielsen, *Black Chant,* 255.

4. Breton, "Second Manifesto of Surrealism," 125.

5. Ibid., 132.

6. Notable exceptions include Eugene Redmond and Barbara Christian. See Redmond's *Drumvoices* (Garden City, N.Y.: Doubleday, 1976). See also Christian's review essay, "There It Is: The Poetry of Jayne Cortez," *Callaloo* 9 (Winter 1986): 235–38.

7. Jayne Cortez, *Mouth on Paper* (New York: Bola Press, 1977).

8. Robert Johnson, "Preachin Blues," *The Complete Recordings* (Columbia 46233).

9. Bessie Smith, "Preachin' the Blues" (Columbia 14195-D).

10. Art Blakey, "Moanin,'" *Art Blakey and the Jazz Messengers* (Blue Note 4003).

11. Davis, *I Got the Word in Me, and I Can Sing It, You Know,* 53.

12. Qtd. in ibid., 52.

13. Winnie Mandela, *Part of My Soul Went with Him,* ed. Anne Benjamin (New York: W. W. Norton, 1984), 112–13.

14. Jayne Cortez, *Unsubmissive Blues* (recording), Bola Press, 1980.

15. Jayne Cortez, "For the Brave Young Students of Soweto," in *Coagulations* (New York: Thunder's Mouth Press, 1984), 44. Subsequent references appear parenthetically in the text.

16. George Frederickson, *White Supremacy: A Comparative Study in American and South African Racism* (New York: Oxford University Press, 1981), 252.

17. Ellison, *Invisible Man,* 27.

18. See Deborah Willis and Carla Williams, *The Black Female Body: A Photographic History* (Philadelphia: Temple University Press, 2002), 59–63.

19. Jayne Cortez, "U.S./Nigerian Relations" (recording), *There It Is,* Bola Press, 1982; Jayne Cortez, "Nigerian/American Relations," *Firespitter* (New York: Bola Press, 1982), 26. All subsequent references to the printed version appear parenthetically in the text.

20. See Evans, *Big Road Blues,* 136.

21. Jayne Cortez accompanied by Richard Davis, *Celebrations and Solitudes,* Strata East Records, 1975.

22. Nielsen, *Black Chant,* 221.

23. One of my own most painful memories about growing up was being lampooned about the size of my lips. In a fit of anger, the self-hatred would spew out, "You liver-lipped bastard."

24. One of the problems presented by cultural texts that revise oral forms is that much of vernacular culture is never recorded. In this case, I must again rely upon my own experiences, having matriculated through high school during the 1970s. My friends and I used this phrase quite often to describe an event that had already taken place.

25. Sterling A. Brown, "Slim Greer," in *The Collected Poems of Sterling A. Brown,* ed. Michael S. Harper (New York: Harper and Row, 1980), 78.

26. For an interesting discussion of Black Arts poetry from a participant's point of view, see Kalamu ya Salaam's "Art for Life." Of course, art rarely leads directly to

the sort of action for which the poets hoped, yet poets like Cortez imbue audiences with sensations that clearly expose the contradictions of everyday reality.

27. This toast was popular in black neighborhoods of the San Francisco Bay Area in the 1970s. My love for toasts like "Dolemite" and "The Signifying Monkey" and my ability to perform them helped me to establish a clearly defined role in my community and marked the beginning of my passion for poetry, although it would take years for me to admit it.

28. Portia K. Maultsby, "Africanisms in African-American Music," in *Africanisms in American Culture,* ed. Joseph E. Holloway (Bloomington: Indiana University Press, 1990), 189. Joyce Jackson, "The Performing Black Sacred Quartet: An Expression of Cultural Values and Aesthetics" (Ph.D. diss., Indiana University, 1988), 161–90.

29. Duke Ellington, *A Drum Is a Woman* (COL 471320–2).

30. Liner notes, ibid.

31. See liner notes, Cortez, *Unsubmissive Blues.*

32. Cortez, *Unsubmissive Blues.*

33. See Sherley Anne Williams, "The Blues Roots of Contemporary Afro-American Poetry," in *Chant of Saints: A Gathering of Afro-American Literature, Art, and Scholarship,* ed. Michael S. Harper and Robert B. Stepto (Urbana: University of Illinois Press, 1979), 124.

34. Ibid., 20 (my italics).

35. Rodgers, "Black Poetry—Where It's At," 7–8.

36. Amiri Baraka, "Black Art," in *Selected Poetry of Amiri Baraka/LeRoi Jones* (New York: William Morrow, 1979), 107.

37. Sanchez, *We a BaddDDD People,* 54.

Conclusion

1. Fenton Johnson, qtd. in Lorenzo Thomas, *Extraordinary Measures: Afrocentric Modernism and Twentieth-Century American Poetry* (Tuscaloosa: University of Alabama Press, 2000), 12. See Thomas's excellent discussion of Johnson in his chapter entitled "Fenton Johnson: The High Cost of Militance," 12–44.

2. Frank Marshall Davis, qtd. in Arthur P. Davis, *From the Dark Tower: Afro-American Writers, 1900–1960* (1974; rpt., Washington, D.C.: Howard University Press, 1982), 122.

3. See Neal, *Visions of a Liberated Future,* 20–21.

4. Sterling D. Plumpp, *Blues: The Story Always Untold* (Chicago: Another Chicago Press, 1989), 78.

5. Amiri Baraka, letter to the author, 28 Sept. 1995.

INDEX

"Negro Characters as Seen by White Au-
    thors" (Brown), 76
The Negro in American Culture (Butcher),
    14
*The Negro in Literature and Art in the
    United States* (Brawley), 3
Negro Poetry and Drama (Brown), 8
Nelson, Red, 40
"Neon Signs" (Hughes), 100
New Negro, 74, 75
New Orleans: black tap dancers in, 1–2;
    Dew Drop Inn, 56; Gentilly Boulevard,
    56; marching-band tradition in, 55; rain
    imagery of, 69; slaves performing music
    in, 70–71
"New Poets" (Walker), 14
"New St. Louis Blues" (Brown), 86
Nielsen, Aldon Lynn, 121, 128
"Nightmare Boogie" (Hughes), 115–16
Nix, Bern, 137
"Nobody Knows the Trouble I've Seen"
    (spiritual), 40
No Hiding Place (Brown), 60
"No Matter, No Matter, the World Is the
    World" (Baraka), 26
"No More Auction Block for Me" (spiri-
    tual), 47, 59
"No Scrubs" (TLC), 52

Odum, Howard, 43
"Odyssey of Big Boy" (Brown), 76–77,
    78–80, 101
"Oh Freedom" (spiritual), 46–47
O'Higgins, Myron, 14–15
"Old Lem" (Brown), 12, 14
Oliver, Paul, 75, 88, 159n40
Olson, Charles, 151n35
"125th Street" (Hughes), 100–101, 117
"One More River to Cross" (spiritual), 59
"on watching a world series game"
    (Sanchez), 34
"Ool-ya-koo" (Gillespie), 62
"Oop-Bop-Sha-Bam" (Gillespie), 62
"Oop-pop-a-da" (Gillespie), 109
Organization of Black American Culture
    (OBAC), 22
"[O]roonie/McVouty" (Gillespie), 62
Oster, Harry, 89
Overstreet, Joe, 19

Page, Thomas Nelson, 76
Palmer, Robert, 44
"Parade" (Hughes), 104–5
Paralinguistic techniques, 66
Parker, Charlie "Bird," 16, 42, 49, 63, 100, 103
"The Party" (Dunbar), 3
Passing, 115
Passing (Larsen), 115
"Passing" (Hughes), 115
Patton, Charley, 43–44
"Perdido" (Gillespie), 62
Petersen, Hector, 123
Pfister, Arthur, 56
*Pisstained Stairs and the Monkey Man's
    Wares* (Cortez), 120–21
"Pleading Blues" (Cox), 40
Plummer, Pamela, 144
Plumpp, Sterling D., 144
Poetics (Aristotle), 34
"Poor Boy Long Ways from Home"
    (Fahey), 85
"Poor Man's Blues" (Smith), 50
Porter, Eric, 98
Pound, Ezra, 96, 99; *Cantos,* 99
Powell, Kevin, 144
Pozo, Chano, 109
"Preachin Blues" (Johnson), 122
"Preachin' the Blues" (Smith), 122
"Precious Lord, Take My Hand" (spiritual),
    30
Profanity in African American music and
    poetry, 23, 131, 150n24
Progressive Labor party, 21
"Projection" (Hughes), 103–4
"Propaganda—or Poetry?" (Locke), 8
"Prove It on Me Blues" (Rainey), 52
Public Enemy, 50
"PUGILISM IN EXCELSIS: The Grinning
    Negro as He Appears to Robert Minor"
    (Minor), 21
Pullen, Don, 50
Pyramid (black poetry category), 26, 27

Racism in Black Arts Movement, 20
Ragtime, 4
Randolph, A. Philip, 20
Rap, 61, 64, 65, 66, 156n102
Rebop, 62
Reconstruction, 48

TONY BOLDEN is an assistant professor of English at the University of Alabama. His articles have appeared in the *African American Review* and *Obsidian III*.

The University of Illinois Press
is a founding member of the
Association of American University Presses.

———————————————————

Composed in 10.5/13 Minion
with Minion & Caravan display
by Type One, LLC
for the University of Illinois Press
Designed by Paula Newcomb
Manufactured by Thomson-Shore, Inc.

University of Illinois Press
1325 South Oak Street
Champaign, IL 61820-6903
www.press.uillinois.edu

R